The DEVONP

DOCKYARD STORY

LT CDR K.V. BURNS DSM RN

MARITIME BOOKS
1984

AUTHOR'S NOTE

The main sources for original documents relating to Devonport Dockyard are to be found amongst the Admiralty records in the Public Record Office at Kew, Surrey; in the British Library's Manuscript Department at Bloomsbury, London W.C.1.; and in the National Maritime Museum at Greenwich, London S.E.10.

The excerpts from Crown copyright records in the P.R.O. appear by permission of the Controller of H.M. Stationery Office; and the plans of the Yard have been re-drawn by permission of the Trustees of the National Maritime Museum.

Most printed sources consulted were available in the Naval History Library in Plymouth Central Library, to the staff of which I offer my sincere thanks for the willing service tendered to me at all times. Peter Ridolfo, Curator of the Devonport Dockyard Museum was also always willing to be of help whenever I needed it.

I am most grateful to the undermentioned for permission to reproduce illustrations:—

    Controller of H.M. Stationery Office for Crown Copyright material

    Department of the Environment

    H.M. Naval Base Photograph Section, Devonport

    Area Photograph Unit, H.M.S. Drake

    Devon Library Services

    The Editors of the Western Evening Herald and Devonport News

    Aero Films Ltd

    S.V.C. Goodman Esq

    Dermot FitzGerald Esq

INTRODUCTION
by
the Rt Hon Dr David Owen MP

Devonport Dockyard has a place in the affections not just of those who have worked in the Dockyard but for many Plymothians, so it is a joy to have collected in one volume much of the story of the Dockyard told in a way which provides information that will not be readily available to many people.

All through history, from Samuel Pepys onwards, politicians have striven to try and improve the efficiency of the Dockyard but the relationship between Parliament and the Dockyard, though concentrating on the need for financial constraint has also been marked by affection and regard for the skills and dedication of the labour force. Time and again Parliamentarians have paid tribute to the Dockyard for it has always been clear that the success of the fleet at sea can never be divorced from its back-up facilities at home. It was therefore appropriate that in the most recent Naval engagement in the Southern Atlantic, generous tribute should have been given in Parliament to the effort and commitment of the employees of the Royal Dockyards. Particularly in responding to the rush of work prior to the sailing of the fleet.

As someone who has watched Devonport Dockyard evolve into one of the most well equipped and modern technological refitting facilities in the world and having seen it from the vantage points of a Plymouth MP, Minister for the Navy and Foreign Secretary, I can only pay my own heartfelt tribute. There are signs that the Dockyards will come under increasing pressure over the next few years with more competition from private shipbuilding yards than it has possibly ever had to face, but somehow the long tradition of service will triumph and my Parliamentary successors will I suspect be dealing with many of the same problems and perhaps like Samuel Pepys be no nearer squaring the circle of serving the fleet and saving money.

CONTENTS

CHAPTER 1

IN THE BEGINNING

The estuaries of the rivers Plym and Tamar, in the broad waters of the Cattewater and Hamoaze respectively, had obviously always afforded a natural protection for vessels of all sizes. It was during the reign of Edward I though that, for the first time, a national fleet assembled at Plymouth. From there 325 ships sailed to Guienne in south west France under the command of Prince Edmund, Earl of Lancaster.

The earliest comparison that can be made of the relative importance of towns from a naval point of view is 1347, the year in which Edward III beseiged Calais and blockaded it from the sea with a fleet of 700 English sailing ships and 37 ships drawn from other countries, including Spain and Ireland. A 'Roll of the Fleet' indicates that Plymouth provided 26 ships and 603 mariners towards that expedition; Fowey sent 47 ships; Yarmouth 43; Dartmouth 31; London 25; Bristol 24; Hull 16; Exmouth 10; Teignmouth 7 and Portsmouth 5.

In 1348 Edward the Black Prince made Plymouth his headquarters for operations against France. Forty ships left the Sound with bowmen on board ostensibly to escort Princess Joan, the Prince's sister, to Gascony on the way to her wedding to the heir to the kingdom of Castille.

On 8 September 1355 he sailed from Plymouth with a fleet of 300 small ships for France "to maintain his father's rights", the local contribution being 25 ships and 203 men. After the Battle of Poictiers — won by the army under the leadership of the Prince — he returned to Sutton Harbour in Plymouth in 1357 with the French King John and many of his noblemen as prisoners.

In 1420 Henry V built the famous ship "Jesus" of over 1,000 tons but even more significant was the fact that during his reign large guns were mounted in his ships for the first time. Henry VII built several ships, amongst them the 'Regent' which, with four masts, was the largest ship yet built in England. However, the ships were still being designed for grappling an enemy and taking her by boarding.

It was Henry VIII who most appreciated the importance of sea power and throughout his reign continued to add to his Navy. His model warship launched in June, 1514 was the 80 guns "Henry Grace à Dieu", or as she was colloquially known, the "Great Harry".

WHY PLYMOUTH?

Many people, and Cornishmen in particular, may sometime wonder why Plymouth was chosen to be a fortified naval port at the entrance to the Channel rather than Falmouth. In the reaches of the River Fal a whole navy might lurk; there was no need to build a breakwater because the entrance was through a channel; and the harbour, with its several inlets, was almost landlocked. Although Plymouth merchants were men of considerable importance in the early 16th century, the town did not achieve any national status until the latter part of the century when it became the principal naval base in the war against Spain. It became a clearing-house for prizes taken at sea, a starting point for voyages of exploration and colonisation and a port of assembly for the Navy.

The choice of Plymouth as the naval base was largely due to Sir Francis Drake whose home port was Plymouth, and to Sir John Hawkins, a native of the town, who was Treasurer of the Navy 1578-89 and Comptroller 1589-95.

State Papers during the reign of Elizabeth I refer to Plymouth as "a port that ought to be fortified" — but how were the necessary means for that purpose to be obtained? It was not, as it is now, within the power of Parliament to vote the funds required. Furthermore, the Queen kept a tight rein over any funds at her disposal.

The means for fortifying Plymouth were therefore obtained in a rather singular way. A tax was levied on the sea harvest of pilchards — so much for the Queen's subjects to pay, but

6

considerably more for foreigners. Drake and Hawkins were sent to Cawsand, on the western side of Plymouth Sound, to investigate and bring the pilchard-curing business from there to Plymouth. The significance of this action will be seen when it is realised that pilchards were much used for the victualling of ships, the sailors thinking them superior to pork. The "pilchard tax" — plus subsidies from some wealthy subjects of the Queen — raised the necessary £5,000 to make Plymouth a fortified naval port.

The question of the choice of Plymouth came to the fore about the time of the Spanish Armada, and naturally those English commanders who had to bear the brunt of the preparations to resist that gigantic naval assault on England, would have a good deal to say as to which port they would make their rendezvous. The decision would therefore rest very much in the hands of the chief sea rovers of the time — Drake and Hawkins, both of whom had personal interests in Plymouth.

It was during the Elizabethan era that the port of Plymouth began to establish for itself the reputation which it has since so proudly maintained as a naval centre. Many adventurers made it their departure point before attempting new voyages of discovery — Sir Walter Raleigh, who sailed to make a settlement in Virginia; Sir Richard Grenville, who set up the first English colony at Roanoke in the area Raleigh had christened Virginia; Sir Humphrey Gilbert who sailed for Newfoundland; and Sir Martin Frobisher and John Davis for the North West Passage. It was from Plymouth's famous Sound that Drake sailed in 1572 on his memorable expedition to Nombre de Dios and again in 1577 on his circumnavigation of the globe. In 1588 120 of the Queen's ships assembled at Plymouth under Lord Howard of Effingham and went to sea on 21 July to engage the Spanish Armada. Where these English ships were built or refitted cannot with any accuracy be ascertained, but being of small size it is probable that several of them would have been built or fitted out at Plymouth.

Sir Walter Raleigh had been fully aware of the admirable advantages that the Hamoaze offered for the establishment of a great naval arsenal and in his work entitled "Excellent Observations and Notes concerning the Royal Navy and Sea Service" he pointed to the objections of confining our Navy to the Dockyards on the Thames and strongly advised that the naval forces should be divided amongst various points around the coast. He also mentioned the commodious harbour which the Hamoaze offered and the ease with which a dockyard could be built there.

During the reign of Charles I, Saltash had been earmarked as a possible site for a new Government dock. Plans were prepared by Sir James Bagge in 1625 but the idea was abandoned after strong objections from the inhabitants and local fishermen who feared for their livelihood.

As early as 1677 there were establishments at Turnchapel and at Teat's Hill, on opposite sides of the Cattewater, for "breaming and repairing" the King's ships, but the increasing dimensions of ships rendered the construction of suitable slips and dry docks essential for these operations. It had, in fact, been contemplated to excavate a dock in the fields inside of Teat's Hill. That same year, 1677, Charles II called for a report on the facilities then existing for the accommodation of the Fleet at Plymouth. He is said to have been impressed with the idea of establishing a Dockyard at Plymouth — "on similar lines to the one at Sheerness".

It is remarkable therefore, that the advantages of Plymouth harbour for the docking of ships were not fully recognised until nearly the end of the 17th century.

A DOCKYARD IS ESTABLISHED

The plans of King James II to introduce French influence into Britain had become so obnoxious that a violent reaction set in against these Catholic conspiracies and finally brought about his exile. Prince William of Orange was imbued with Protestant instincts and a hatred of France — so had everything in his favour. On 5 November 1688, he and his wife Mary, daughter of James II, landed at Brixham. The tyranny of King James II was over, and on hearing of William's arrival, Plymouth immediately declared for him as King, one of the first towns in the country to do so.

Towards the end of the month, the great fleet of several hundred ships which had brought William and Mary to England, left Brixham and sailed to Plymouth where it received a great welcome. The fleet remained at anchor in the Cattewater during the winter and in the spring of 1689, King William joined his ships there and set sail for Ireland later. Undoubtedly it was during this visit to Plymouth that William authorised the scheme for the new naval dockyard to proceed.

At that time ships of war lying in Plymouth Sound were entirely at the mercy of what scanty docking accommodation was available in private yards. This did not satisfy the aspirations of William of Orange, and an Act of Parliament was passed "investing certain powers for the purchase of such lands as were thought necessary within the Barton of Mount Wise and the parish of Stoke Damerel, for the use of His Majesty and his successors, for the defence of the Dockyard, shipping in harbour, etc."

Plymouth was considered an advanced store base in June, 1689, and before the end of that month a Storekeeper had been appointed. His instructions were "to muster the ships there as well as to serve stores until the Yard shall be settled and a Clerk of the Cheque established".

In August, the Admiralty, for the first time, mentioned the possibility of building a dry dock somewhere within the Plymouth harbour limits. There were then no Government docking facilities west of Portsmouth, and even there, the old dry dock, which alone could take the largest man-of-war, was fast becoming useless through moisture and decay.

In the Hamoaze, 150 sail of the line could be moored in safety and such was the depth of water that the largest ship in the Navy could come into harbour at any state of the tide with all her guns and stores on board. There was also a rise and fall of tide amounting to about 19 feet on the average spring tides which would be of great service in the docking and undocking of ships.

POINT FROWARD

Plymouth Sound and the various inlets of the Hamoaze and Cattewater were surveyed in the autumn of 1689 by Edward Dummer, who had once been in charge of the facilities at Teat's Hill. At this time though, he was Assistant Master Shipwright at Chatham, destined to become Surveyor of the Navy in 1692. His report suggested Point Froward, at the entrance to the Hamoaze, as the most suitable site for building a dock. Dummer's choice was soon approved and the Government ordered the Navy Board to put the arrangements in hand for building a single dry dock capable of taking a third rate, using the contours of the land to aid construction.

In March 1690, a Portsmouth mason, Robert Walters, put in a tender of £11,000 for the work and guaranteed that he would complete it within fifteen months. A few months later though it was again proposed that a dock should be built in the slate quarry near Saltash Ferry. As in earlier years, this proposal was also turned down, and on 3 December, 1690, the contract was signed with Walters.

Immediately after the formalities were completed, Dummer put forward a more ambitious design. Instead of building a dock which could only take a third rate or below, he proposed a larger dry dock supplemented by a wet basin. The basin would enable ships to be sent into the dry dock more easily than from an anchorage in the river; would make the refitting of ships easier; and would also protect the dry dock from the full effects of the prevailing westerly winds.

The following extract from a report by Edmund Dummer, Surveyor of the Navy, to the Admiralty in December, 1694, sets out some of the advantages of a wet basin:—

"Therefore where the offices of triming and repairing ships shall bee executed where men and materialls are ready at hand and under a constant eye of comand and boats, as so many theives, quite laid aside and the ship itselfe brought to hand and sheltered even from weather itselfe, that worke which usually takes up five weeks done in open harbour may for ought I know bee capable of dispatch in as many days by means of this basin; for so soone as the sailers' part is done and the shipp dock'd, the floating and hanging stages are immediately brought about her to dispatch the upper workes, much sooner done thus floating than in the dry dock by reason men will hang about a ship with a smaller provision and care than in the dry dock, as being less sensible or affraid of falling into water halfe that height which they are subject to in the other place besides the difference of the matter they shall fall upon and the shores and other things than may take them up in their falling, wherefore it is not to be doubted but the taking off this care

"Where it all began — Point Froward"

will add more agilitie to the workman to ply his true business."

"Now by this convenience, I will presume to say such works where shipps do not require grounding may bee done for a third less charge in point of wages, infinitely less in time, because strength may bee augmented and lessened to any proportion readyly and by the advantage of materialls lying neare and sheltered from weather, the worke itselfe shall bee more effectual in all respects."

The revised plan was approved, subject to King William's personal direction that the dry dock should be large enough to hold a first rate. The work was again contracted to Walters, but obviously the estimated cost had now very much increased — from the original £11,000 to a revised one of £21,887. 14s. 8¾d. Estimates for residences, stores, workshops, etc. (each quoted to the last farthing) were added and the grand total "happened" to come to exactly £50,000.

FIRST DOCKYARD OFFICERS

The first Dockyard Officer appointed was, as mentioned above, the Storekeeper, joined soon afterwards by the Master Attendant and Master Caulker. A Boatswain and a Carpenter, serving aboard a ship in Plymouth Sound, were appointed to also serve in the Dockyard.

On 18 January, 1691, Elias Waffe became the first Master Shipwright of the Yard, remaining there for the next eight years. He was soon followed by a Clerk of the Survey, and by the end of the year Captain Henry Greenhill, R.N., had become the first Commissioner.

The annual salaries of these officers were:—

Commissioner	£400
Storekeeper	£120
Master Attendant	£100
Master Shipwright	£100
Clerk of the Survey	£60
Master Caulker	£60

Where all the workmen came from is not known. In January, 1692, they were mustered for the first time when the total was just 74.

FIRST WET BASIN AND DRY DOCK

Froward Point was about two miles from the Victualling Offices and remote from Plymouth itself. The site comprised two fields held by a Mr. Doidge and Sir Nicholas Morice, and a third contained within the Barton of Mount Wise. Sir Nicholas was the younger son of Sir William Morice, Bart., whose father — also Sir William, who represented Plymouth in Parliament and was a former Principal Secretary of State and Privy Councillor to King Charles II — had purchased the Manor of Stoke Damerel from Sir Edward Wise for the sum of £11,600 in the year 1667. Sir Nicholas succeeded to the title and estate because the elder son William, had died before him. He died in 1725 and was succeeded by his only son, Sir William.

At this time Sir Nicholas was just a boy of thirteen. The Admiralty had signed a contract with the builder before contacting any of the owners of the land involved. When the lad's trustees were informed, they replied that an Act of Parliament would be required to sell the property, and that meanwhile, no building was to take place. The boy's guardian was a Hamburg merchant, obstinate and bad-tempered, who at one stage threatened to remove any stores that the Admiralty might send to the site. No Act was passed and the work carried on but it was not until May, 1694 that the dispute was finally settled by the Admiralty paying young Morice £139 for the damage done to his property. Eventually a lease was signed by which the Navy rented the land at Froward Point for seven years at £100 a year.

By the end of 1692 the wet basin and dry dock had been completed and they were put into use the following year. The basin, about 256ft x 200ft, could take two first rate ships and the dry dock, 40ft 6 ins x 170ft, could take one. They represented a great advance on anything previously built in this country. Both dock and basin were built on artificial ground, about four acres of new ground having been reclaimed from the river. The dock — very nearly saucer-shaped — was built of Portland stone with steps cut in the sides which enabled a ship to be supported more easily than in earlier docks with wooden slopes.

Two sets of gates were fitted; one set at the riverside of the basin where the entrance was 50 feet wide, and the other set between basin and dry dock. By closing them at appropriate states of the tide it was possible to contain the water within the basin and dry dock at high tide; or, alternatively to drain the dock after it had received a ship from the basin. There were no pumps in those days suitable for emptying docks, but the provision of a culvert connected with the river, would drain the dock or basin by gravity as the tide receded. The particular form of lock gates — in two halves — enabled them to be moved by just five or six men compared with the eighty or so required to move the larger single gate in use at Woolwich and Chatham.

The basin was bounded on each side by jetties, which were platforms projecting over the water and supported by wooden pillars.

OTHER BUILDINGS

In the year 1692 William III again inspected the Dockyard site and the pressing need for increased facilities caused Parliament to include in their vote for the Navy for the next twelve months a sum of £23,406 for "finishing the Yard at Hamoaze", including dwelling houses for officers; storehouses and workshops; and to enclose the Yard with a wall. Between 1694 and 1697 this work proceeded but by a new contractor, one named Fitch.

One of the first buildings to be completed was a large central storehouse or "Magazine" as Dummer called it. This 60ft square store was the pride of the Yard. Two stories high and in the form of a hollow square, it could hold the equipment for forty men-of-war. Standing on a point of land it could be approached at any state of the tide on at least two of its four sides. It was described as "something beyond what is to be found in any of the Magazines in the other Yards", and for four years it remained the only storehouse of note.

A salient feature of the original layout of the Yard was the precision and symmetry with which residences for the officers were constructed on the centre line of the dock and basin. These residences formed what was originally known as "The Walk" but later became "The Terrace". They were sited about ninety feet above the general quay level and commanded a most imposing view of the Yard. A brick wall passed along the front of the whole building making a large terrace about 400 feet long.

The site of the first dry dock

The officers occupying the houses, from north to south, were as follows — the more modern designations being given in brackets where appropriate:—

Chirurgeon (Senior Medical Officer)
Master Caulker
Shipwright's Assistant (Senior Constructor)
Clerk of the Survey (Superintendent Civil Engineer)
Master Attendant (Admiral Superintendent's Secretary)
Master Shipwright (Constructive Manager)
Commissioner (Admiral Superintendent)
Clerk of the Cheque (Cashier)
Storekeeper (Superintendent Naval Stores Officer)
Clerk of the Ropeyards (Master Rigger)
Master Rope Maker
Master Boat Builder
Boatswain of the Yard

The design of the Yard was well planned, with most buildings sited in a logical order although compressed into a small area. The hemp- and rope-houses stood together near the main store. Nearby was the sailroom sufficiently far away to allow a sail-drying area. Then came the yarn and spinners' houses, and to the south stood the rigging house.

The ropehouse at this time ran in an east to west direction and was no less than 1,056 feet long and 25 feet wide. The western end nearer the river was joined at right angles by the Hemp House, which was 102 feet long x 44 feet wide. This house fulfilled other functions — the first floor being used as a sail loft and the second as a mould loft where lines of a ship's hull could be laid out to full size.

A very important side of the rope-making was the tarring of the yarn warped from the spinner. The rapid rotting ropes made from white yarn indicated that it was necessary to treat it with tar before it was made up into cordage. For this reason there were additional buildings, the White Yarn House and the Tarred Yarn House, with a Wheel House in between. The wheel was mounted

The Terrace

over the tar bath, or 'tar-kettle' as it was called, so that by being turned by men who walked inside it, the white yarn was drawn through the tar and passed to the Ropehouse for twisting into cordage.

The ropemaking establishment at Plymouth was to become of great importance to the Royal Navy, for in later years it was to make almost half the ropes they used.

Masthouses were conveniently sited near the shore line, where timber could lie in the mud. There were also two graving places within the 24 acres occupied by the Yard. On these graving slips — one each side of the Wet Basin — a ship would often be hove up, bottom cleaned and tallowed, and launched again the same day.

AN ORGANISED GUARD

The need to protect this area saw the introduction of an organised guard — derived from the force of Porters, Warders, Rounders and Watchmen that was first introduced into other Royal Dockyards in 1686 by Samual Pepys, the then Navy Minister. The Porters controlled entry into the Yard and directed visitors; the Warders were responsible for the keys and security of buildings; the Rounders were the roving patrolmen; and the Watchmen were employed to keep an eye on the ships and storehouses. The Porters, Warders and Rounders were all permanent staff but the Watchmen were taken from gangs of men looking for work who used to wait outside the Dockyard gate each evening hoping to be selected. The first Porter at Plymouth was a John Perry who was engaged on 1 January 1693 and served until he died on 10 July, 1718.

Instructions to the Watchmen included the regular ringing of bells, the bells being so situated as to prevent the Watchmen remaining in their sentry boxes beyond the prescribed time. In later years, when war was almost continuous and prisoners were being brought home to be then accommodated in ships in the Hamoaze and employed in Government establishments, the Guard was supplemented by military personnel.

Punishment for anyone convicted of an offence, no matter how insignificant it may seem, was severe. Captain Philip Vanbrugh, Commissioner of the Yard from 1738-53 records in his journal (P.R.O. Adm.174/288) that on the evening of 23 January, 1741, William Wallin, a boy, was whipped at the gate for stealing two iron bolts valued at 1/6d.

FIRST SHIPS BUILT

From its inception, ships were being refitted in the new Dockyard and within twelve months of completion, the Yard had begun its own shipbuilding programme and the first two ships had been launched. They were two 73 tons advice boats "Postboy" and "Messenger", launched on 3 April, 1694. At the same time, work had been progressing with Dockyard labour on the fourth rate "Anglesea", 48 guns, which was launched a fortnight later from the yard of a Mr. Fint. The annual estimates for 1694 (P.R.O.7/169) include a cost of £20 "to Mr. Fint for the hire of the yard where the fourth rate is being built", and afterwards "the fifth rate", which must have been the "Lyme" launched on 20 April, 1695. The building of all these ships was supervised though by the Master Shipwright of the Yard, Mr. Elias Waffe.

The first ship of any size actually laid down in the new Dockyard was the fifth rate "Looe", under instructions contained in a Navy Warrant dated 28 March, 1695. She was added to the Navy in August, 1696, but six months later, 30 April, 1697, the "Looe" had the misfortune to run against a rock near Baltimore in Ireland and was lost. Fortunately, all the ship's company was saved.

In April, 1695 the Navy Board was asked by the government "what number of ships, from 60 to 90 guns, may be set up and built in a reasonable time in any part of England." For Plymouth they reported that "in His Majesty's Yard at Hamoaze is one dock and in Cattewater one slip, fit for such purposes. From whence it may be gathered that Plymouth is qualified for building four such ships at a time."

By 1697 the place was working as a well-equipped Dockyard — the only Dockyard built specifically to meet the needs of the time.

BEGINNINGS OF THE TOWN OF PLYMOUTH DOCK

By the end of the 17th century the proposal to purchase the land on which the Dockyard was being built had still not materialised. For a number of years, the land continued to be leased from Sir Nicholas Morice and Mr. Doidge. These landlords had also been unwilling to allow the erection on the surrounding land, of houses for the workmen.

During Captain Greenhill's period of office as Commissioner of Plymouth Yard (1691-95) most of the artificers employed in the Yard were accommodated on board a man-of-war or hulks in the river. The alternative was a trudge from the Yard to the nearest houses in Plymouth — at that time just an area around Sutton Pool and mostly within the town walls — two miles or more from the Yard. There was hardly any accommodation available in the vicinity of the Yard.

In 1692 a communication was sent to the Lords of the Admiralty by Captain Greenhill setting forth the claims of the men for facilities nearer their place of work. A further submission was made in January, 1697 to the Hon. Edward Dummer, Esq., who by that time had become the Surveyor of the Navy. The following is an excerpt from it:—

"Honoured Sir,

If the difficulties which our workmen undergo, by living too far from their business, were not of very great prejudice to His Majesty's service, and a fatigue to them almost intolerable at this time and season, we should not trouble you again herewith, you having yourself taken notice of it, and know it to be absolutely requisite to be redressed."

"For it is now almost three years that the services of the Navy have been performed at this Yard, and in these new docks, and the inconvenience and discouragement to the people who have attended thereon have been often complained of, but this winter seems to have made all our avenues and passes thereto much more rotten and troublesome than we have observed them formerly, which induces us to be more earnest to invite you to the remedies the nature of them requires, namely, that the persons who are employed here, may have liberty to build habitations near their business."

The unwillingness of the landlords to permit buildings being erected in the vicinity of the Yard was finally overcome when, in 1700, the first houses of what was to become the town of Plymouth Dock, were built at North Corner.

Building continued northwards to form Cornwall Street and Cannon Street and within fifty years of the establishment of the Yard the population of Plymouth Dock had grown to half that of the town of Plymouth and by the end of 100 years its numbers had equalled it.

Cornwall Street ran down at right angles to the river front and divided the northern end of the Yard from land which had been taken over and rented by the Ordnance Department. The War Department acquired this 4½ acre site in 1718 for the purpose of a Gun Wharf. The land, leased from Sir Nicholas Morice, was held on the same terms as the Dockyard at an annual rent of £11. 17s. 6d. and a fine of £35. 12s. 6d. on every seven years renewal. The buildings erected therein, to the design of Sir John Vanbrugh, needed considerable excavation but were completed within seven years. There were two principal storehouses, three stories high, for muskets, pistols, grapeshot and other small stores; sheds for gun carriages; a powder magazine; and a cooperage. Between 1720-23 a row of houses was built therein for the Senior Officers. The bulk of the construction work was carried out by a London stonemason, William Cowley, with Abraham Curtis being responsible for the wood-work.

The area was known as the Gun Wharf until 1941 when it became Morice Yard and integrated into the Dockyard.

DOCKYARD CHAPEL

To meet the spiritual needs of the workmen, a Chapel was erected in the north-east corner of the Dockyard near the entrance. Over the south door was placed the following inscription:—

"In the 11th year of the reign of King William 111, Anno Domini 1700, this Chapel was founded and built by the generous and pious contributions of officers and seamen belonging to a squadron of men-of-war paid off in this Yard (after ten years expensive war with France), being propagated and carried on by the industry and religious endeavours of George St. Lo, Esq., Commissioner of the Yard and Comptroller of the Pay."

The building originally consisted of a tower and one aisle, but another aisle was added by the Rev. Robert Hughes, Chaplain of the Yard 1765-93, on condition that he received the emoluments arising from the letting of the pews. On 15 July, 1786 an agreement was reached between Rev. Hughes and the Lords Commissioners of the Admiralty which released him from any claim to the emoluments. The Government compensated Rev. Hughes and the following year appropriated the Chapel for the exclusive use of the Navy and the Dockyard.

The money he had spent on the Chapel was returned to him; he was granted a regular stipend paid by the Government; and he also received 2d. a month from the pay of each of the officers and men belonging to the ships laid up "In Ordinary", i.e. In Reserve.

OTHER WORK IN THE YARD

In the Yard, work other than the normal shipbuilding and repair was also undertaken. When the condition of a ship could not be overcome by

(a) ordinary repairs, which constituted an annual caulking and tarring of the bottom, repairs to masts and yards, and making good other defects; or

(b) extra repair, which entailed a thorough overhaul of equipment and renewal of decayed timber;

the ship, if it was found to be economical, would be re-built. This consisted of virtually taking the ship to pieces and building in to a new one as much of the old wood as was still serviceable. The new ship did not always receive the same name nor was a new ship always built in the same Yard as that in which she had been taken to pieces. The proportion of re-built ships was considerable and in the early 18th century amounted to almost one third of the ships in the Navy.

In October, 1707, the Navy Board expressed concern at the large number of shipwrights and caulkers borne in Plymouth Yard and yet so little ship-building was being done. The Commissioner stressed that the new ship then building — the fourth rate 64 guns "Plymouth" which had commenced building more than two years earlier — was only to keep the workmen employed when there were no ships to refit. Captain Greenhill, who was then in his second term of office at Plymouth (1704-08), pointed out that when a ship came in, all hands could, if necessary, be taken off the new ship. He was careful to issue a local order to his officers to ensure that the above routine was actually carried out.

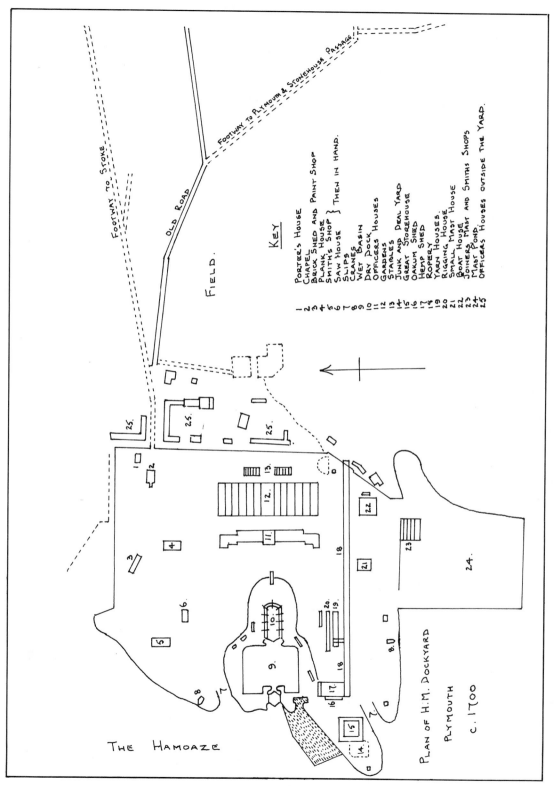

THE HAMOAZE

FIELD.

KEY

Porter's House — 1
Chapel — 2
Brick Shed and Paint Shop — 3
Plank House — 4
Smith's Shop — 5
Saw House — 6   } Then in hand.
Slips — 7
Cranes — 8
Wet Basin — 9
Dry Dock — 10
Officers Houses — 11
Gardens — 12
Stables — 13
Junk and Deal Yard — 14
Great Storehouse — 15
Oakum Shed — 16
Hemp Shed — 17
Ropery — 18
Yarn Houses. — 19
Rigging House. — 20
Small Mast House — 21
Boat House — 22
Joiners Mast and Smiths Shops — 23
Mast Pond. — 24
Officers Houses outside the Yard. — 25

Footway to Plymouth & Stonehouse Passage

Footway to Stoke

Old Road

Plan of H.M. Dockyard
Plymouth
c. 1700

The early days were not without their difficulties. Captain William Wright, Commissioner at Plymouth in 1703-04 and again from 1708-11 wrote in October, 1710 that "three times they had endeavoured to dock the "Assurance", a 70 guns third rate, but had not had water enough, and therefore had been obliged to careen her".

CHAPTER 2

EXPANSION

In 1727 the first enlargement to the Yard took place when another portion of land was rented to the Admiralty by Sir William Morice, son of Sir Nicholas. The new area, which increased the total area of the Yard from approximately 35 to 54 acres, was used partly as a Mast Pond and partly as a Timber Ground. Around three sides of it were built large mast-and boat-houses. Running westwards was a Camber — a long canal about 70 feet wide — which besides connecting the Pond to the Hamoaze also gave access to a Mud Dock and to two slips formed on the northern side of it. The Mud Dock, as its name implies, was left dry at low water, but at other times could be used for unloading timber. The Timber Ground was connected to the rest of the Yard by a bridge under which small boats, masts and spars could pass to the Mast Pond beyond.

By the 1740's the adjective "old" was being applied to the original dry dock, to distinguish it from a second dock which was then being built to the north of it at the head of one of the original graving slips. Between May, 1740 and February 1741, a dam was built half-way down the slip to enable work to be carried out on the erection of dock gates. These were completed on 19 September, 1741, and work commenced on 1 December 1742 on the slopes and parapet walls of the dock. Completed twelve months later, the first ship taken in to this new dock, named North Dock to distinguish it from the original No. 1 which became South Dock, was the "Chichester", 80 guns, to have her bottom "breamed to kill the worm".

North Dock was soon extremely busy with ships entering and leaving almost daily after having had their bottoms cleaned. A ship could be in the dock and another taken on to the slip astern but, obviously, the first ship could not then be undocked.

This combined North Dock and graving slip was later converted to form a Double Dock, one of the first of its kind to be constructed in this country.

With gates fitted at mid-length and at the riverside, it was possible to use the two parts — Head Dock and Stern Dock — separately. The dimensions were:-

Head Dock	Width at coping level	52 feet
	Length between gates	200 feet
	Depth from floor to cope	26 feet
Stern Dock	Width at coping level	52 feet
	Length between gates	190 feet
	Depth from floor to cope	25 feet

THE ROPEYARD

In 1743 officials in the Plymouth Ropeyard reported that "stores were overflowing" and proposed that the men's working week be reduced to 1½ days. However, the Navy Board told them to keep it to 2½ days in order to supply Portsmouth's needs. Two years later, when it was decided to increase the number of apprentices in the Government roperies — one new boy for every eight ropemakers — the men objected violently. They wished to limit their numbers because they felt that when the war ended the surplus ropemakers would be turned out without any hope of alternative employment. They refused to accept the new apprentices without a fight. Strikes started at Chatham, then spread to Woolwich and Plymouth. During May, 1745, three of the four naval ropeyards were at a standstill. A similar strike had occurred at Woolwich in 1729 when the ropemakers were successful with their demands. In 1745 the men quoted the earlier incident as a precedent, but to no avail. The Admiralty called for troops to quell the disturbances. They discharged the ring-leaders and "pressed" as many as possible and put them aboard a man of war.

WARTIME 1739-48

During the war of 1739-48 the Plymouth Yard possessed two dry docks and three building slips. With these facilities the Yard turned out a remarkable number of new and re-built ships, including six fourth rates each carrying 50-60 guns.

The only significant addition made to the Yard during this period was the enlargement of South Jetty at a cost of £4,858, a project which had actually been ordered and initiated before hostilities commenced.

In the same period the work force increased rapidly — at a greater pace than any other Yard. The Navy Board, at first, viewed this with concern because it doubted whether sufficient timber could be obtained to keep so many shipwrights occupied. The supply of timber was a problem that was to occur frequently throughout the era of wooden fighting ships.

Towards the end of the war though, when the services demanded of Plymouth were growing rapidly, the Yard actually found itself short of shipwrights and caulkers. Therefore, in November 1747, a recruiting drive was made along the South coast and to places further north. The terms offered were so good, that men came to Plymouth from as far away as Liverpool and Hull.

When peace was declared in 1748, all the available mooring spaces in the Hamoaze were occupied by ships "In Ordinary". Forty eight ships were paid off at Plymouth and the Navy Board gave instructions to the officers of the Yard to stop working extra hours until further orders. On 5 July, 29 riggers, 49 rigger labourers and 20 others were discharged, followed the next day by 42 joiners, 39 house carpenters, 101 labourers and 39 others.

After a visit to Plymouth by the Lords Commissioners of the Admiralty in August, 1749, more men were ordered to be discharged, including 59 shipwrights, 40 caulkers and 24 smiths.

UNION DOCK

In 1758 a plan (P.R.O. Adm.140/174) was produced for the construction of another dock upon the site of the slip immediately north of the Double Dock. This was known as Boyne's slip after the ship of that name, the last of the 70 guns class of ship which was begun in the Yard on 9 August, 1758 and launched 26 May, 1766.

However, to obtain sufficient clearance from the Double Dock, the proposed new dock had to be moved about 30 feet further to the northwards (P.R.O. Adm.140/219).

It was eventually completed to receive its first ship, the "Union", 90 guns, on 17 March, 1763; hence its name Union Dock. The dock 239ft. 4ins. long, 86ft. 7ins. wide and 26ft. 10ins. deep, was faced with Portland stone but had granite blocks to support the shores necessary to dock a ship.

"NEW GROUND"

On November, 1761 it was approved to enlarge the Yard southwards by another 10 acres (P.R.O. Adm.140/149) forming an area known as "New Ground", a term which survived to modern times. This brought the total area of the Yard to 70 acres.

Upon this additional area, three acres of which were reclaimed from the river, were built three building slips. These were completed within ten years. Another graving place was also built on the shore, north of the Camber, adjacent to the Great Storehouse.

Much of the remaining area was taken up with additional Masthouses and a Mastpond. The Pond was enclosed from the river by a very strong wall, 10 feet thick and about 380 feet long. The water entered through two openings about 40 feet wide over which were light wooden bridges.

THE FIRST SLIP AT MUTTON COVE

About 1763 at the southern limit of the Yard, a slipway was built "for the unloading of furze", a type of brushwood which was used in the process of "breaming" — cleaning a ship's bottom by burning off. This operation was performed with a ship in dock or by laying her aground and allowing the tide to ebb from her. Men then held kindled furze, faggots or reeds to the ship's bottom which, by melting off the pitch that covered it, loosened whatever filth or weed that may have adhered to it. In August, 1774, plans were drawn for a building slip to be built on this site next to the boundary wall (P.R.O. Adm. 140/221). The cost of this undertaking was £1,056. 1s.6d. for materials and £834.6s.8d. for labour — a total of £1,890.8s.2d. Further alterations were

The West Prospect of His Majesty's Dockyard, near Plymouth 1736

made to this building slip in 1788 "for getting up cutters, etc. for repair" (P.R.O. Adm. 140/222).

SOUTH DOCK

To make room "for shifting a knee of the head of a ship repairing", temporary excavations had been made to the head of South Dock — the original dry dock. Pursuant to a Navy Board Warrant dated 18 September, 1776 (P.R.O. Adm. 140/178) permanent arrangements were made to these works in the dock — "to tidy them up" — by making a flight of steps half way down on the middle line at the head of the dock, with small slopes on each side continuing to the floor of the dock.

THE ROPERY RE-SITED

A stumbling block to the extension of the Yard southward had been the Ropehouse which had been built in an east-west direction at what was the original southern extremity of the Yard. With the extension taking place, this building acted as a barrier to communications between the ends of the Yard. It was essential therefore that the Ropehouse be re-sited.

The opportunity was taken after a disastrous fire on the night of 2/3 July, 1761 when about 500 tons of cordage, 700 sails and 1,000 tons of hemp were destroyed in a sea of flame.

By 1768 two buildings, each 1,200 feet long, were planned to be built in a north-south direction at the eastern boundary of the Yard as far away as possible from the wharves. On 27 August, 1773 Messrs. Templer and Parlby entered upon a contract to build these new ropemaking and associated buildings. The two buildings were identified as the West and East Ropehouses; the westerly one being used as a Laying House and the easterly one as a Spinning House. Also built to the eastwards of these Houses were the four associated buildings — a White Yarn Store; a Tarring and Wheel House (the motive power centre for the tarring process); and two Tarred Yarn Houses.

At much the same time as the Ropery was re-sited many of the original storehouses and worksheds were demolished and replaced with new. The Great Storehouse which had existed almost since the Yard began, was pulled down and a new block erected between the Camber and South Dock.

LOCAL FORTIFICATIONS

For the defence of the Dockyard and shipping in the harbour, special Acts of Parliament in 1758 and 1766 sanctioned the raising of fortifications within the Barton of Mount Wise and the parish of Stoke Damerel. A wall and trench would surround the town as well as the Dockyard, excepting "only two common ways or passages to the water at Mutton Cove and North Corner" — exceptions which were to prove a handicap to future Dockyard expansion. The plans, prepared by a Mr. Smelt, provided for three gates each with a drawbridge across the trench, forming the North Barrier at New Passage Hill; Stoke Barrier at the end of Fore Street; and one at Stonehouse Hill. Little work on the ramparts and ditches — which became known as "The Lines" — was done before 1810. Having been condemned as unsuitable by the Duke of Wellington in 1816, they were left incomplete for nearly forty years. In 1853 work on "The Lines" was resumed as part of the inner ring of defence along with the chain of forts proposed to be built from Tregantle to Staddon around the then Three Towns — Plymouth, Devonport and Stonehouse.

BIGGER SHIPS

The first 98 gun second rate ship built in Plymouth was the "Duke", laid down in October, 1772 and launched in 1777. During the period of her construction, the Yard reached the summit of its capabilities when the 100 gun first rate "Royal Sovereign" was laid down in 1774. She covered herself in glory at the Battle of Trafalgar, wearing the flag of the Second-in-Command, Vice Admiral Cuthbert Collingwood. At one stage she was engaged single-handed with several of the enemy. The "Royal Sovereign" was severely damaged, but after the action made for Gibraltar where she underwent temporary repairs and was jury-rigged for the voyage back to Plymouth, where she arrived in January, 1806.

POWDER MAGAZINE AT KEYHAM

In 1784 a Powder Magazine was built at Keyham Point. It held 20,000 barrels of powder and was supplemented by "powder hulks" — former men-of-war — moored in the Hamoaze. It

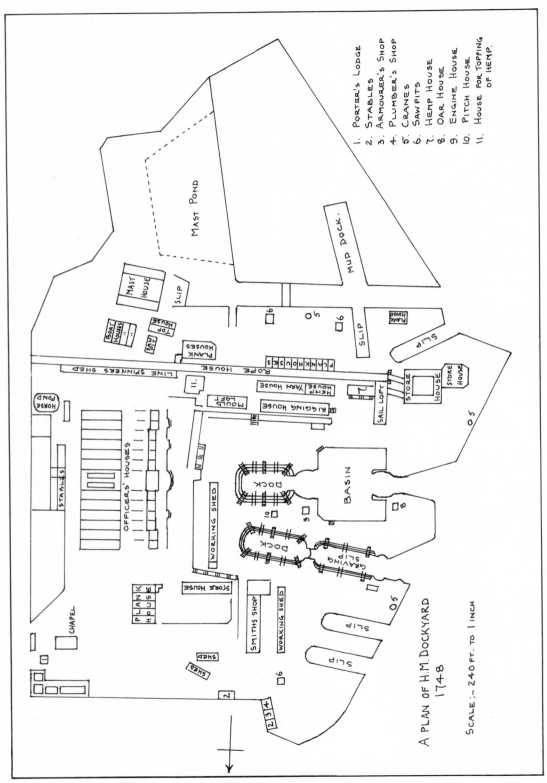

A PLAN OF H.M. DOCKYARD
1748

SCALE :— 240 FT. TO 1 INCH

1. Porter's Lodge.
2. Stables.
3. Armourer's Shop.
4. Plumber's Shop.
5. Cranes.
6. Sawpits.
7. Hemp House.
8. Oar House.
9. Engine House.
10. Pitch House.
11. House for Topping of Hemp.

was completely isolated from other facilities and consisted of several detached stone buildings erected with every precaution taken against accidents, lightning or fire. The whole of the depot covered a space of about 5 acres. A neat row of houses was provided therein, built specifically for the workmen.

In 1821, a terrible explosion occurred in this Magazine, the noise of which was reported to have been heard in Liskeard nearly fifteen miles away.

About 2 p.m. on a Friday afternoon in January, the Receiving House of the Powder Works blew up. A quantity of three-pounder cartridges had lately been received which the men in the establishment were opening and putting the powder and shot into separate barrels. Happily seven members of staff had that day been sent to measure timber half a mile away, and only two remained. Unfortunately, both of these persons — an old man named Carne and a boy called Matthewson — were killed.

It was conjectured that in throwing the iron shot together, some sparks occurred and, communicating with the loose barrel, caused the fatal explosion. About forty barrels were in the house, which blowing up at the same time, spread great destruction and violently shook houses for several miles around. At Saltash, and even in Plymouth, many panes of glass were broken, and some of the shot were picked up at St. Budeaux.

NEW UNION DOCK

In 1789 another dry dock, to be called the New Union or North New Dock, was completed. Designed by the architect Mr. Parlby, it was again built not exactly on the site of a former slipway but between two of them — the northernmost one named as Medusa's slip and the next one south named as "the one on which the "Anson" was built". (P.R.O. Adm. 140/154 dated December, 1784). The "Medusa" had been launched on 23 July, 1785, but the slip had continued to be known as "Medusa's Slip". The "Anson" was on the building slip which bore her name for almost eight years before being launched on 4 September, 1781. The new dock was therefore built between, but encroaching across, the Medusa and Anson slipways.

During construction the Admiralty, by an Order dated 16 November, 1785, directed that this dock should be lengthened at the head by ten feet (P.R.O. Adm. 140/180) and the clearance over the sill of the dock gates increased by a foot to 27ft. 6ins. The New Union Dock then became one of the largest docks in the country — the length from the gates to the head of the dock being 250 feet and the breadth 85ft. 3ins.

Whilst this dock was under construction King George 111, who subsequently performed the dock's opening ceremony, visited the site. His Majesty observed that the planned dimensions had been exceeded and enquired the reason why. He was told that the dock had originally been designed to take the longest vessels then in the English fleet — the "Queen Charlotte" and the "Royal George" — but that as the French, then our old and well-established enemies, were building at Toulon a much larger ship than either, the dock had been altered for her reception. Oddly enough this impudence was justified by the result — that very ship, the "Commerce de Marseilles", 120 guns and 2,747 tons, being the first ship to enter the dock!

It was in commemoration of this Royal visit that the little building on King's Hill — or Bunker's Hill — was erected. It stands on top of a natural outcrop and is approached by a winding path which passes a "grotto" and an ornamental fountain. The tablet on it records "This building was erected in the year 1822 to perpetuate the recollection of the visit of H.M. King George 111 of blessed and glorious memory and of His Majesty's admiration of the rock on which it stands and the scene around."

OTHER GREAT SHIPS

The first 80 guns ship built with two decks was the "Caesar" which began building at Plymouth on 24 January, 1786 and was launched on 16 November, 1793. She was on continuous sea service until December, 1813 when she was taken in hand to be fitted as an Army Clothing Depot ship. She lay at Plymouth until February, 1821 when she was broken up in the North New Dock.

The most famous ship to leave the Yard before the end of the 18th century though, was the "Foudroyant". Designed on similar lines to those of an earlier French ship of the same name, the 80 guns third rate "Foudroyant" — the second of the new class, ("Caesar" being the first) — was launched on 25 May, 1798. For twelve months from June 1799 she was the flagship of Lord Nelson, but her active life ended on 30 November, 1812. She remained in Harbour Service at Plymouth until 1851 when, after repairs, she became tender to the gunnery ship "Cambridge". In January, 1891 she was sold out of the service to Mr. J. Read, Jnr., of Portsmouth, for £2,350, but later he accepted an offer of £4,000 for her from a German firm. The public outcry caused by this sale inspired the formation of a syndicate to recover the ship from the German purchaser at a price of £6,000 — a sum forthcoming through the generosity of Mr. Wheatley Cobb of Caldicot Castle, near Chepstow. The ship was towed back to the Thames and was restored to her original state by Mr. Shuttleworth of Erith, using the plans loaned by the Admiralty.

The refit was to cost about £20,000 so to recover some of these expenses it was decided to exhibit the ship at various sea-side resorts — visiting Plymouth in September, 1896. When at Blackpool in June, 1897, the "Foudroyant" broke from her moorings and ran ashore near the North Pier, to become a total wreck. A Birkenhead man bought the wreck with the intention of making it one of Blackpool's sideshows but further heavy gales in November dashed the ship to pieces. In August, 1898 the embedded wreckage of the "Foudroyant" was cleared using explosives.

DISASTERS OF THE 18th CENTURY

The history of the Yard during the 18th Century would be incomplete without recording some of the disasters that occurred during that period. A great tempest struck the area on 26 October, 1760 which dismasted several ships in the Sound. A strong sea was running when the "Conqueror", 70 guns, commanded by Captain Lloyd, was driven on to the eastern end of St. Nicholas Island (later Drake's Island). Her mainmast and mizzenmast were cut away and some of her guns thrown overboard, but all to no avail and she became a total wreck.

The fire which destroyed so much of the Ropehouse in 1761 was thought to be the work of an arsonist. At least two other attempts at arson were frustrated by vigilant sentries. James Aitken, known to his associates as "Jack the Painter",

made two unsuccessful efforts at getting over the Dockyard wall to set fire to buildings inside. He earlier had been more successful at Portsmouth where he got in and set fire to the Ropery. He had come to Plymouth seeking further infiltration but to no avail. He was eventually captured and in 1776 at Winchester was tried and, pleading guilty, was sentenced to death.

On 14 December, 1798, the prize "La Coquille" which had been captured from the French, off the coast of Donegal, was lying in the Hamoaze when, at about 4 p.m., fire broke out in the after part of the ship in the vicinity of the Gunroom. Within five minutes an explosion blew up her quarter deck, her mizzen mast fell over the side and flames spread along her main deck. As she was surrounded by other ships she was cut adrift from her moorings and towed to South Down on the Cornish side of the Hamoaze, where she grounded on a mud bank. The "Endeavour", a brig of Scarborough, carrying coals to Guernsey, was secured near "La Coquille". She too caught fire and both ships were totally destroyed.

It was on the 22 September, 1796 though, that the most deplorable disaster ever known in the port occurred. The frigate "Amphion" had received instructions to proceed on a special mission and farewell dinner parties were being given on board by the officers, and wives and sweethearts were "exchanging their boisterous pleasures" with the sailors on deck. Her commanding officer, Captain Israel Pellew, and his First Lieutenant were dining with Captain William Swaffield of the "Overyssel". The officers were seated together at table and a servant was just entering the cabin with a dish when a sudden and violent shock threw them from their seats. Pellew rushed to the deck where he saw his ship's foremast being carried into the air. A block struck and partially stunned him. Both he, and the Lieutenant were saved but Captain Swaffield was crushed to death in the wreckage. About 300 persons were believed to have perished. Mutilated bodies and torn wreckage drifting down the harbour with the tide were soon all that was left of the gallant ship and her company.

The cause of the disaster was never ascertained though suspicion was directed towards a dishonest Gunner who, it was suggested, dropped a light amongst some stolen ammunition.

Captain Pellew remained in a critical state for some time and ever afterwards bore the mark of the blow he had received. After a brilliant career he died on 19 July, 1832, aged 73, and was buried in Charles Church, Plymouth, where a tablet was erected to his memory.

Early in October, an attempt was made to weigh the "Amphion", and two frigates "Castor" and "Iphigenia", were moored on each side of her. It only served to renew the feelings of the inhabitants when putrid bones were dislodged and cast on shore all along the beach. In November, however, Mr. Hemmings, the Yard's Master Attendant, succeeded in dragging the wreck to the jetty to be broken up.

As a means of preventing a repetition of such an accident it was ordered that every ship should henceforth land her powder before entering harbour.

CHAPTER 3
PAY

The daily rates of the workmen's pay remained unchanged for the first eighty years of the Yard's existence. They varied from 1/1d. a day for a labourer to 3/- a day for a shipwright. In addition, shipwrights, caulkers and other tradesmen were paid a lodging allowance of 2½d. a week.

From March to October there was a 12 hour working day, from 6 a.m. to 6 p.m., with half an hour for breakfast and one hour for dinner. In the winter months, working hours were from dawn to dusk. Then no time was allowed for breakfast but the men continued to get their hour for dinner.

Although men were working long hours for six days a week, they were always willing to add to their meagre incomes by working as much overtime as they could get. Indeed, the authorities frequently authorised the working of overtime during times of high food prices to enable the men to meet the rising cost of living.

Overtime could be worked as "tides" or "nights" — a "tide" being a period of 1½ hours and a "night" a longer period of five hours. The payments were 7½d. for a "tide" and 2/1d. for a "night". Unfortunately the overtime was not always properly supervised and measured, with the inevitable result that it left itself open to abuse. For instance, in 1710, a clerk in the Yard claimed, and was paid for, 94 "nights" and 151 "tides" in a single quarter. Obviously, it was nigh impossible for him to have worked that number of extra hours.

"CHIPS"

The men supplemented their pay through the much abused perquisite known as "chips". The authorised procedure allowed each man to take out of the Yard — under his arm — a bundle of the odd ends of wood he had cut off during his day's work. However, this privilege was always being abused. Large pieces of timber were often cut up solely for the purpose of providing "chips". The workmen also claimed the right to carry the bundles, tied up, on their shoulders. In this way other valuable materials such as copper and brass, would be concealed and carried out through the Dockyard gate. The privilege was abolished in 1801 and cash was paid in lieu, ranging from 6d. a day for shipwrights to 3d. a day for labourers. Thereafter the "chips" were sold at auction once a fortnight.

VARIOUS METHODS OF PAYMENT

In the 1770's the Admiralty adopted "payment by results" for the shipwrights. It comprised five different methods based on the principle of incentive — task work; piecework with unlimited earnings; piecework with limited earnings; day work; and classification.

Task work meant that the hull of a ship was divided into twenty five stages of construction and a price agreed for each stage in each class of ship. This method of work was voluntary and only the best men volunteered for it and selected the other men they wanted in their squads.

For piece work the hull was divided into all its component parts down to the smallest of jobs, such as driving a bolt, and each item of work was measured. This brought about, in 1809, the formation of a separate department of qualified measurers.

Day work did nothing to improve productivity but under "classification" the men were paid the rate commensurate with their productivity; therefore the best workers could earn a bonus but conversely the worst suffered a pay cut.

DISCONTENT OVER PAY

All these various pay schemes caused a great deal of suspicion amongst the men whose feelings on more than one occasion boiled over into sufficient discontent to cause a riot.

In 1799, a considerable number of men stormed the Dockyard gates which were normally closed during working hours. The gates were battered down, the rioters spilled out into the town and violent clashes occurred with the military. John Pollexfen Bastard, who represented Devon in Parliament from 1784 until his death in 1816, without waiting for any requisition, marched his regiment, the East Devon Militia, into the Yard and brought the rioting to an end. For his action, Bastard received the thanks of the King.

After thirteen weeks of confusion, order was restored and the malcontents returned to their work after concessions had been made by both sides. Immediately after this incident, guns were sited at the Dockyard gates.

In 1801, during a period of some famine when prices soared, the authorities tried to tighten up on the "Task and Job" rates. The reactions amongst the men were worse than it had been some years earlier. They rampaged through the Yard, broke open the storehouses and transported large quantities of provisions and stores out to the town. There they sold their loot to any person who could afford to buy. It was almost a month before the authorities were forced to compromise. To alleviate the men's distress — "during the present high price of provisions" — they were granted additional payments. Men with four children were allowed an additional 1/- a day; those without children an extra 6d. a day; and proportionate payments for varying sized families.

In 1803 a Naval Commission enquiring into the method of payment in the Dockyards approved Task Work but denounced Piecework. They recommended a return to Day Work for the repair of ships. Three years later, the Commission recommended that new schemes should be drawn up by a Committee of Master Shipwrights. This Committee produced a single piecework scheme for both the building and repairing of ships, and this was introduced in 1811.

Once the American War of 1812 was over, the Admiralty discontinued both Task and Piece Work. This annoyed the shipwrights and some of the best of them departed to the private yards on the Thames. So Task and Piece Work was re-introduced but with a limit on earnings of 3s.4d. a day in the summer and 2s.8½d. in winter.

Piece Work came under further criticism so it was discontinued altogether in 1833. Another system of Classification was introduced, the three classes being paid 4s.6d., 4s.0d. or 3s.6d. a day. However, the men detested this system, so in 1842 that too was discontinued, and Day Pay was substituted for everyone. This routine lasted until 1847 when another method of payment was tried, that of "Day Work and Check Measurement". Under this system each man's work was measured as if it had been done on Piece Work but if it failed to reach a proper standard of quality or quantity a deduction was made from his wages. On the other hand if his work reached the required standard or was above it, nothing was added to his wages. Obviously the system was intensely disliked, except by the large numbers of Work Measurers created to administer the scheme.

A system of Task and Job Work with unlimited earnings was then pursued in the Dockyards but was abolished on 31 March, 1857. The wages of the shipwrights were then increased by 6d. a day and joiners, painters and coopers by 4d. No addition was made to the wages of smiths, millwrights, sail-and rope-makers, while the wages of labourers were actually reduced from 14/- to 12/- a week.

PAY ROUTINE

Until 1805 it had been the practice to calculate the earnings of the workmen at the end of each quarter. By the time the books were properly adjusted, it was always near the end of the succeeding quarter before the payments could be made, so the men's earnings were always at least three months, sometimes four to six months, in arrears.

The procedure is typified by the following messages which the Commissioner Captain Greenhill, sent to the Mayor of Plymouth requesting that "they be fixed in some proper place at Plymouth and the same notice given by the Crier throughout the town."

"This is to give notice that on Wednesday, the 18th June at 6 o'clock in the morning, I shall begin the payment of this Her Majesty's

Yard for the Midsummer and Michaelmas Quarters Anno Domini 1706" — dated 16 June, 1707;

and

"This is to give notice that on Thursday next at 7 o'clock in the morning I shall begin to pay wages for Christmas Quarter 1706 and Lady Quarter 1707" — dated 13 January, 1708.

The consequences of this delay in payment was that the men were entirely beholden for the subsistence of themselves and their families on the local shop or tavern keepers, who supplied them with what they wanted on credit, but at a deduction of from 10 to 15 per cent less than what was shown on his earnings certificate issued by the Clerk of Cheque's office. The workmen were therefore subjected to a deduction in the rate of his earnings of at least two shillings in the pound.

The money was usually brought around by ship from Portsmouth. To actually pay it out, was a long drawn out affair even though there was only about 1,000 employees. Commissioner Philip Vanbrugh's journal (P.R.O. Adm. 174/288) records that payment on 17 June, 1742 lasted from 7.15 a.m. until 2.45 p.m. and was continued the next day from 7.15 a.m. to finally complete it at 11.15 a.m.

On the first Saturday of October, 1805, a new mode of payment was adopted throughout all the Dockyards, whereby each man was paid, in cash, from $3/4$ to $7/8$ths of the amount of his week's earnings, under the category of "subsistence", while the remainder went to account, to be calculated at the end of the quarter under the category of "arrears".

It was August, 1813 when it was announced that in future the full wages would be paid weekly.

CHAPTER 4

LAUNCHING HIGHLIGHTS

The launching ceremony in the days of England's wooden walls was an event of no small importance, and a phenomenon in the annals of Plymouth Dockyard occurred on 17 November, 1804, when the launching of the first rate "Hibernia" and two frigates "Circe" and "Pallas" took place within an hour and a half on the same afternoon.

The "Hibernia" had been under construction for twelve years during which time she had been lengthened by having an eleven feet section inserted in her amidships. After an eventful sea-going career, she was fitted out at Devonport in 1855 to become a Receiving Ship at Malta. There, for about forty years, she wore the flag of successive Admiral Superintendents of Malta Dockyard, before being finally sold for £1,010 at a public auction in 1902.

The "Circe", a fifth rate of 32 guns, had a short but distinguished career before being sold out of the service in 1814. The "Pallas" had an even shorter life because in December, 1810 she became a total wreck in the Firth of Forth. Captain Lord Cochrane first commissioned the "Pallas" and needing men for this new ship, used the unbelievably low trick of a "press" on Christmas Day. He naturally fell foul of the law and was summoned to appear before the local magistrates. He did not appear but sent a letter. Held to be in contempt of court, a warrant was issued for his arrest, but before it could be enforced, he was at sea. He cruised for a month off the Azores taking several valuable prizes, one with about 430,000 dollars on board. The "Pallas" — the "Golden Pallas" — returned to Plymouth in April, 1805, bearing a golden candlestick nearly five feet high on each of her three mastheads. The case against Lord Cochrane dragged on in the High Court for nearly two years, and although Plymouth won its case, the town never seems to have recovered its costs.

FIRE IN THE EASTERN ROPEHOUSE

On the night of 16 November, 1808, a dreadful fire broke out in the Hemp House near the southern end of the Ropehouse. It burned for three hours, from 11 p.m., but was eventually controlled by Dockyardmen and ships' companies landed at North Stairs from ships in the Hamoaze.

Nearly four years later an even greater disaster to the rope-making facilities occurred, when, at about three o'clock on the morning of Monday, 8 June, 1812, a fire broke out in the Eastern Ropehouse. It was so fierce that it was feared it might threaten other parts of the Yard. Nearly five hours elapsed before the fire was under control.

The fire was believed to have "burst forth" from several parts of the Ropehouse at the same time, particularly at the extremities of the 1200 feet long building. There were not many stores therein but the fire destroyed, or badly damaged, much of the machinery used for twisting cables.

Watchmen and military sentinels were examined on oath but it could not be ascertained whether the building was fired by overheated hemp; by lightning; or by incendiaries. During the investigation, the finger of suspicion pointed to a person who was in the town of Plymouth Dock a few days previously to the fire and had left on the fateful Monday morning for Torpoint. From thence the suspect was believed to have taken a chaise towards Falmouth.

In consequence of reports that the fire was an act of incendiarism, the Admiralty sent to Plymouth Dock, Mr. Jones, a solicitor, and Mr. Lavender, the Bow Street officer, to make further enquiries. These finally revealed that

(a) fire had broken out only in one place — on an attic floor of the store containing ropes and hemp;

and (b) the suspected cause was that on the day previous to the fire, lightning had flashed very strongly on to the building.

The fire destroyed over 900 feet length of the Ropehouse and had caused about £15,000 worth of damage.

The Ropehouse was re-built by 1815 to a fireproof design prepared by Edward Holl, Architect to the Navy Board.

WATER SUPPLY

Water, supplied by the Plymouth Dock Water Company, was first brought into the Yard in 1797, but it was not until 1812 that it was piped around the Yard. That year a reservoir, elliptical in shape 70 feet long, 60 feet broad and 8 feet deep, was built near the Dockyard gate in the garden of the Master Shipwright. This reservoir was soon found not to hold enough water, so another was built in part of the Commissioner's garden between the gates and the officers' stables.

LOSS OF THE "CAPTAIN"

About 11 o'clock on Friday night, 22 March, 1813, the third rate "Captain" 74 guns, — Nelson's ship when he captured the "San Josef", 112 guns, at Cape St. Vincent in February, 1797 — caught fire. The fire was first discovered in a small galley under the forecastle, but how it started was never discovered.

The "San Josef" had recently been converted into a hulk and was actually lying alongside the "Captain", discharging stores prior to being docked. The lashings between the ships were cut and the "San Josef" was moved to a safe distance. The "Captain" though was not so fortunate. Fearing that she would drift when the fire came to the bitts that held the mooring chains, the shipwrights of the Yard drove large clamps into her bow and ring-bolts through her stern to which chains were attached. An assortment of boats then attempted to tow her to the western side of the harbour. All attempts to scuttle her failed because of the intense heat. Two field pieces and carronades were brought near to her in dockyard launches and used to fire nearly 200 shots at intervals along the ship's side. These penetrated between wind and water but had no effect on letting water into the ship to put out the fire. As the ship burned, the "Captain" became more buoyant and the shot holes remained above water.

About 4 a.m. when the ship had burned almost to the water's edge, her bow gradually dropped, the water poured through her port-holes and the "Captain" majestically glided to the bottom.

DOCKYARD CHAPEL RE-BUILT

By 1814 the Chapel's condition had deteriorated to such a dangerous state that it was decided to pull it down and erect a new one on the same site. The order for its demolition was issued in September, 1814. On 11 November, the Chapel tower, with the aid of ropes around its upper part, was pulled crashing to the ground.

The first stone of the new Chapel — designed by Mr. Adams of Stonehouse — was laid on

The Summer House on King's Hill

Thursday, 19 January, 1815. There was no ceremony but the name of the Commissioner of the Dockyard, Robert Fanshawe, was engraved on the stone. Soon afterwards it was discovered that the ground had not been properly prepared for the new building, it being composed of loose rubble, which on examination occupied the cavity of a quarry dug, it was supposed, when the original Chapel had been built. This delayed completion of the new Chapel but it eventually opened for Divine Service on 9 November, 1817, the minister then being the Rev. George Jope.

The new Chapel — a handsome building of hewn stone, 100 feet long, 76 feet wide with towers 85 feet high — was capable of seating 2,000 persons. The seats were nearly all appropriated — the nave for resident officers and their families, with the senior ones at the front then diminishing in seniority, and with their families at the back. In the gallery, naval and military officers sat facing the pulpit, with the band and choir behind them; each side was set apart for the use of sailors and marines who were duly marched and marshalled into their places. (P.R.O. Adm. 140/234).

Said to have cost £24,000, the Chapel, unlike the original, was paid for by the Government. It

The New Dockyard Chapel

was the only Dockyard Chapel that possessed a peal of bells, these having been cast by Pennington of Lezant in Cornwall. Charles Bellman, John Winter and John Dyer of Plymouth Dock carried out the contract for the plaster work and Thomas Selden performed the glazier's work (P.R.O. Adm. 174/300).

During the period of the demolition of the old Chapel and the building of the new, Divine Service was held in one of the Ropehouses.

CHAPTER 5
COVERING THE DOCKS AND BUILDING SLIPS

The premature decay of wooden ships had frequently been considered but it was more with a view to complaint rather than to any demonstration of remedies. Some observations on the latter subject were presented on 28 November, 1811 to the Rt. Hon. Charles York, then First Lord of the Admiralty, by Richard Pering, Clerk of the Cheque in Plymouth Yard. In the April following he published them as a 78 page pamphlet entitled "A Brief enquiry into the causes of premature decay in our wooden bulwarks with an examination of the means best calculated to prolong their duration."

Pering's father was a country gentleman who for many years was an officer in the South Devon Militia of which regiment he was a Lieutenant Colonel when he died. He placed son Richard under the direction of Sir John Henslow, who had then lately retired from Surveyor of the Navy and had become one of the Commissioners of the Navy Board. By 1811 Richard had been in H.M. Service for nearly thirty years — "the longest standing as a principal officer of any of the individuals in the different Dockyards, except one or two" — so he felt well qualified to pass on his comments.

He first recommended that the shipwright should be properly educated in naval mechanics before being permitted to undertake the performance of any duties in the Dockyard.

"Within the last twenty years more improve-ments had taken place than in any previous comparable period of time. Unfortunately,

there was a dearth of persons, properly qualified by a regular system of education, to undertake duties in Dockyards. Training was organised for military personnel at Woolwich, but how different was the manner in which young men were brought up for the Royal Dockyards. Boys, previously bound apprentices to the Master Shipwright for a set period, are placed under the eye of some common men who, however unfit for the task, are called Instructors. Yet they take no other account of their pupil than that of seeing them attend to their work in order that they themselves may not lose the allowance given by the government."

The author then proceeded to attribute the premature decay of our ships to the use of unfit materials and the improper methods of building, fastening and caulking.

"By the present mode of shipbuilding, a first rate becomes useless from premature decay in five or six years and the average duration may be said to be limited to eight years."

One of the causes of rapid decay he attributed to the immense quantities of foreign timber which had been introduced into the Dockyards.

"Foreign timber should be used by itself and not inter-mixed with English oak. Greater emphasis should be placed in growing home timber. Some public spirited persons have exerted themselves in such planting, particularly J.P. Bastard, M.P. for Devon."

Pering next condemned the use of treenails — pieces of cleft wood one foot to three feet six inches in length, made round about $1\frac{1}{2}$ inches in diameter. He defied all the shipwrights in the country to invent a worse instrument for confining the planks of a ship to her side, even though it was, and ever had been, the standard practice in this country.

"A treenail, being rather smaller in the middle than at the ends — made so by the workmen in order that it may be driven easily — never fills the hole into which it is driven. Consequently, if ever it admits water at the outer end which, from shrinking, is liable to do, that water immediately gets into the middle of the plank, if not further."

"A ship would then soon be left without fastenings. Many ships have gone to the bottom and thousands of lives lost from this mode of fastening. How common it was to hear a sailor say that a vessel must have "sprung a butt" before foundering. In warm climates, treenails shrink; timbers separate from planks and planks from timbers, both inside and out, with the treenails disengaging from both".

Pering therefore recommended that treenails should be substituted by bolts made of copper, which itself was preferable to iron. Copper need only be 7/8" in diameter so that every plank and timber would be less wounded than by the 1½" hole required for a treenail. The copper bolts would also be ten times stronger and would never decay. "However, prejudice may suggest that the cheap cost of treenails and iron should give them preference over a metal so scarce and costly as

Interior view of the slip at Mutton Cove

copper".

"The treenail is the second thing to decay" he said, "the first being the oakum".

The caulking of seams required the insertion of two threads of oakum per one inch thickness of planking and the means of doing it created another problem.

"Work starts at top-side and proceeds downwards. If a seam is not wide enough, the reaming irons of the caulker must make it so. As the caulker works downwards, the whole strain of the preceding strake lies on the treenails of the next. Is it any wonder that treenails should be upset, or the planks fly from their work?"

Pering suggested a progressive method of caulking. The first four or five seams should be 'half caulked,' then return to finish the first seam; half caulk the sixth; then finish the second seam, etc.

The common method of fastening knees, beams, etc., was by driving in bolts, the projecting heads of which were then clenched. After docking for partial repair, a ship would go out again with some of her bolts having been renewed, whilst others, worked slack by racking, etc., remained. The new bolts therefore had to bear most of the strain.

"These bolts should be replaced by screws" Pering observed. Another problem highlighted by him was the presence of dry rot.

"Dry rot, whose origin was attributed to damp, cannot be easily eradicated from a ship once it has taken root. It may be partially suspended by fire or heat — but it can only be exterminated by the removal of the affected timber."

"After a ship has stood twelve months in frame to season, she is then planked, her upper deck laid and caulked. In this state it is taken for granted that she must be kept dry. But during this period of planking and caulking, some of the timber must, to a greater or lesser extent, be exposed to the elements or be affected by evaporation from the planks which had been boiled in steam kilns for one hour for every inch thickness. During this procedure, about 1lb of water was absorbed by every cubic foot of timber. The very thing intended to prevent the formation of dry rot, unavoidably creates it."

"It is partial leaks, suffocating damp and oozing drips, or where there is no circulation of air to dry the timbers, that produce it. Why is it different now to the past? Formerly, timber intended for shipbuilding was collected and seasoned for a considerable time before being wanted."

He therefore recommended that all our ships should be built under cover. Ships had been known to stand in frame for ten to fourteen years, to season; a most unreasonable period, as was proved by the decay found in many of her timbers before the ship could be proceeded with.

"A ship built in the dry would season more in one year than present ships do in five, as fungi would have no opportunity to form. The workmen would also be under cover. There would be no need to hurry to lay the upper deck to form a shelter."

In 1785 the "Royal Sovereign" had been launched at Plymouth with a housing over her, open at both ends, and attached to the ship. The "Argonaut", while afloat, had a covering placed over her which was also open at both ends. In both cases the 'through draught' was found to be so injurious that it became necessary to remove those temporary protections.

Pering proposed that not only should ships be protected by housings whilst building, but that the greater part of the dry docks should also be covered over. He thought it would cost about £10,000 to house over one ship, but was so confident with his suggestions that he advocated that, as an experiment, one ship be built in the way he proposed.

"Let her remain on the slip, and I have no hesitation in saying that she would be sound at the end of 200 years. Let all our ships be framed, planked and caulked in the dry; let them be fastened with copper; let a screw be employed instead of a clench; let ships be built under cover and remain so to season; let foreign timber be expelled from our Dockyards — unless it be of equal quality to English oak; let no caulking iron be permitted to approach any part of a ship till she is in a proper state for launching. Ships would then last three times as long as they do now."

Pering repeated that he had nothing to fear from his construction. He had not launched out into a boundless sea of speculative opinions, to bewilder himself and readers in a maze of plans without use or without explanation, but everything he said was founded on facts — "incontrovertible facts ascertained during a long course of daily, almost hourly, observation of every particular."

He ended though, with a note of bitterness, saying that his ideas and plans will be regarded with envy by some who think well of no scheme, however advantageous, not projected by themselves.

The following year he published a further pamphlet "On the preservation of the British Navy when in a State of Ordinary". Its early pages though were devoted to further comments on the reaction to his first pamphlet.

"Temporary coverings made of canvas, and tarred, have since my recommendations of them, been raised over all the docks in Plymouth Dockyard devoted to the repair of ships. If they had been constructed in a proper manner though, the danger from fire would have been much lessened."

To add weight to his protests about fastenings, Pering also described how on 2 March, 1811, the "Clara", a Spanish frigate, had been taken into dock in Plymouth Yard to be fitted for a Receiving Ship. After the water had receded, the plank actually dropped from her bottom, "which would not have happened if her fastenings had been of copper."

In the period 1775-1784, 66 men-of-war foundered or were lost at sea, along with 11,080 men. What occasioned these disasters? "Chiefly, bad fastenings."

He then offered a few suggestions for the "effectual preservation of the British Fleet in Ordinary".

"The mode heretofore, was for ships to be dismantled, paid off, and placed "In Ordinary" after preparation by the Dockyard. The decks are opened to allow air to circulate freely. In this condition they lie at moorings. Thus they are left to moulder away and soon get decayed."

"Docks are not so much wanted as covered slips. Every slip in the Royal Dockyard ought to be covered over. No ship should be permitted to remain afloat if it can be avoided. Therefore, the first thing to consider is what is the best way of providing slips for such ships as can be "hauled up". Then, if they are opened in different places for ingress of air, planks will shrink and a ship will become dry, and continue to be so until required for service, a little before which she should be closed up and caulked."

"Numerous methods have been tried to discover a speedy method of seasoning timber by artificial means; such as stoving, charring, burning in sand, coating with compositions of various kinds, etc., and also to destroy the principles of vegetation by different chemical preparations — all, as far as I know, have failed."

More criticisms were heaped upon Pering which caused him to again go into print when, in 1814, he published:-

"A Reply to some strictures in the Quarterly Review (No. XIX) on Indian built ships; to which he annexed economical recommendations for effectually preserving the British Navy on the return of peace whereby millions of money may be saved to the Country."

In this work he replied to some of the criticisms of his statements on the failings of treenails; the quality of timber being used; and the need for covering ships under construction and/or repair. Pering remained adamant that if his plans were followed "the British Navy might be kept sound, dry, healthy, durable and always ready to start at a moment's notice."

He again quoted the case of the "Royal Sovereign" on which he said "a humble attempt was made to protect her by placing a canopy made of deals covered with tarred paper extending from stem to stern attached to the fabric with which she was launched. This covering most certainly prevented the sun from rending her decks but it was not far enough extended laterally to protect her sides from the drifting rain nor altogether from the falling drip. It was attached to the ship after she was complete in the year 1785 and removed in September, 1787. A similar roof made at the present period might cost about £3,500. Had the slip on which she was built been covered over prior to her commencement, the early decay which followed for want thereof might have been prevented; many of her timbers were found rotten and shifted, previous to her plank being brought on, and after the ship was completed it was discovered that a part of her keel, deadwood, floor and first futtock were likewise rotten, and obliged also to be shifted, of which I was an eye-witness. A more expensive ship I do not believe was ever built; fortunately her durability has, in a great measure, expiated her original cost, which I attribute to her being built principally with sound, well-seasoned English oak, having in her construction but little timber of foreign growth. Although the "Royal Sovereign" has, since she was launched, received considerable repair, it must be allowed she has proved a durable ship, and what has contributed also to her durability has been the short period she was covered both when on the slip and after she was launched."

Mr. Pering's suggestions were to revolutionise the scene in Plymouth Yard. The first ship to which his plan for permanent covers over ships repairing was applied, was the 74 guns "Spencer" which went into dock on 18 October, 1811, where she remained under a temporary covering — made of canvas and tarred — until 21 January, 1814. In the April, the first rate "St. Vincent" which was preparing for launching on 4 June, 1814, was ordered to season on the slipway, under cover, in the manner recommended by him. She was eventually launched on 11 March, 1815.

In February, 1815, a covering, shaped as an inverted triangle, was placed over No. 1 slip — the northernmost one — on which another first rate "Britannia" was being built. Later Nos. 2 and 3 slips were covered, but with a mansard roof, a roof with two contiguous slopes where the lower is steeper than the upper. In 1820 No. 1's roof was altered to a similar shape as that over Nos. 2 and 3.

Eventually all the building slips and dry docks, except the New Union Dock, had large roofs erected over them. It was necessary for one dock to remain uncovered so that in an emergency a ship could be docked with her masts standing. The roofs not only covered the ship but also sheltered the workmen employed on shore preparing timber.

The Head Dock was described as being "within a noble permanent shed" with a slated roof studded with 142 windows. It was 263 feet long, 49 feet 9 inches high and had a span of 134 feet. The last roof over a dock — the Union Dock — was removed in 1876.

Mr. Pering's plan for "hauling up" ships on to slipways, thereby overcoming the shortage of docks, was accomplished with small ships at first, but in July, 1817 the 74 guns "Kent" 1,964 tons, was hauled up.

In February, 1819, his plan for covering ships "In Ordinary" was also adopted. These covers, of a removable pattern, costing £300 each, were placed over ships as they left a dock after undergoing repairs.

CHAPTER 6
ROYAL EVENTS

A noteworthy event took place on 4 July, 1814, when the Dockyard mechanics with their officers, organised a procession to commemorate the establishment of peace. The procession was formed "in order", each branch being preceded by the emblems of his trade in the shape of models, and carrying the appropriate tools. Even Mr. Cox, the rat-catcher, displayed his "trophies" that had been captured in the Dockyard.

On 8 September, 1831, a similar procession took place in honour of the Coronation of King William IV and His Royal Consort Queen Adelaide. The men formed up in the Dockyard, then passed through Fore Street, St. Aubyn Street, and George Street, to parade at Mount Wise in front of the Government and Admiralty Houses. From there they proceeded through the north-east barrier gate to Stonehouse, through Union Street into George Street, Plymouth — then Bedford Street, Old Town Street, into East Street and back to the Dockyard, passing the Royal Naval Hospital at Stonehouse en route.

Their Royal Highnesses — as the Duke and Duchess of Clarence — had visited the Dockyard in 1828 to attend the launch of a first rate of 104 guns. This ship had been laid down as the "London" but when launched on 28 July, 1828, in the presence of the Lord High Admiral, the Duke of Clarence, the Duchess named the ship "Royal Adelaide".

After commissioning in 1835, this ship spent four years in the Hamoaze wearing the flag of the local Commander-in-Chief. Then for twenty years she lay 'unemployed' until, in 1859, she became Guardship for the Ordinary. In 1891 the flag was transferred to "Vivid" (ex-"Capercailzie", an iron screw yacht) and in August of that year the "Royal Adelaide" made the first of the only two voyages of her life when she was moved to Chatham to be used as a Receiving Ship. In 1904 she was condemned; on 4 April, 1905 she was sold; and in June, 1905 sailed to Dunkirk to be broken up — the first and only time she had been in a foreign port.

SECOND SLIPWAY AT MUTTON COVE END OF THE YARD

A plan dated 14 February, 1816 (P.R.O. Adm. 140/224) was prepared for the construction of a second slip at the Mutton Cove end of the Yard "suitable for building 74 guns ships or repairing frigates". The southern end of the Mast Pond was to be filled in and the Pier, used for the landing of Furze ever since the slipway for such a task had been replaced by the southernmost building slip, was also to be taken away.

A contract dated 29 March, 1816, was signed with George Hartrup Brocket of Woolwich, and other contractors, for building the slip, and for excavating some of the rock of Whitehouse Hill to prepare a site for a steam kiln. The slip, the final plan for which was dated 29 April, 1816 (P.R.O. Adm. 140/225) brought the number of building slips to five, they being numbered, at that time, 1 to 5 from the north to south.

DIMENSIONS OF DOCKS AND BUILDING SLIPS

The dimensions of the docks and building slips at this time are set out in a manuscript in the Public Record Office at Kew — "Plans and Midship sections of Docks, Basins and other Building Slips at Plymouth in His Majesty's Dockyard (P.R.O. Adm. 140/189). The essential details were as follows:-

North New Dock (or New Union Dock)

(a) Length from gates to top of slope at head
    252ft. 0ins.
(b) Length from gates to bottom of slope at head
    214ft. 0ins.
(c) Breadth at upper stone altar amidships
    95ft. 10ins.
(d) Breadth at bottom of dock amidships
    41ft. 0ins.
(e) Breadth at piers of gates
    56ft. 6ins.
(f) Depth of dock amidships
    27ft. 11ins.

North Dock (or Union Dock)

(a) 240ft. 10ins; (b) 201ft. 0ins; (c) 99ft. 0ins;
(d) 44ft. 8ins; (e) 56ft. 2ins; (f) 27ft. 7ins.

Head Dock

(a) 222ft. 5ins; (b) 196ft. 9ins; (c) 81ft. 0ins;
(d) 45ft. 5ins; (e) 52ft. 6ins; (f) 25ft. 1½ins.

Stern Dock

Gates to Gates 192ft. 2ins. (c) 80ft. 0ins.
(d) 48ft. 7ins; (e) 52ft. 4½ins; (f) 25ft. 1½ins.

South Dock

(a) 197ft. 3ins; (b) 168ft. 8ins; (c) 71ft. 7ins;
(d) 40ft. 3ins; (e) 50ft. 4½ins; (f) 22ft. 5ins.

Boat Basin (No. 1, the original Wet Basin)

Extreme length from North to South 253ft. 9ins.
Extreme length from East to West   197ft. 0ins.
Depth   24ft. 0ins.

The Entrance tapered from inside of wall, 53ft. 8ins., to outside of wall 50ft. 6ins.

Graving Slip

(a) Depth at Jetty aft   18ft. 8ins.
(b) Depth at Head   17ft. 10ins.
(c) Length along the floor   169ft. 0ins.
(d) Length to top of slope   189ft. 6ins.
(e) Breadth at top   72ft. 3ins.
(f) Breadth at bottom   58ft. 6ins.

No. 1 Building slip

(a) 16ft. 10ins; (b) 6ft. 0ins; (c) 197ft. 6ins;
(d) 208ft. 7ins; (e) 66ft. 0ins; (f) 49ft. 9ins.

No. 2 Building slip

(a) 16ft. 10ins; (b) 6ft. 0ins; (c) 195ft. 9ins;
(d) 206ft. 7ins; (e) 67ft. 0ins; (f) 50ft. 4ins.

No. 3 Building slip

(a) 17ft. 4ins; (b) 6ft. 1ins; (c) 197ft. 1ins;
(d) 207ft. 6ins; (e) 68ft. 0ins; (f) 50ft. 0ins.

Plan of H.M. Dockyard c.1821

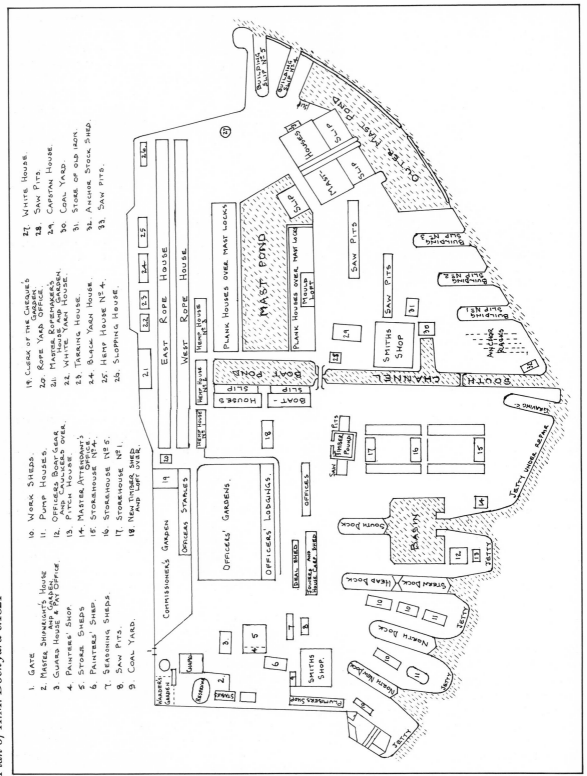

1. Gate
2. Master Shipwright's House and Garden.
3. Guard House & Pay Office
4. Painters' Shop
5. Store Sheds
6. Painters' Shed
7. Seasoning Sheds.
8. Saw Pits.
9. Coal Yard.
10. Work Sheds.
11. Pump Houses.
12. Officers Boat Gear and Caulkers over.
13. Pitch House.
14. Master Attendant's Office.
15. Storehouse No. 4.
16. Storehouse No. 5.
17. Storehouse No. 1.
18. New Timber Shed and Loft over.
19. Clerk of the Cheque's Garden.
20. Rope Yard Office.
21. Master Ropemaker's House and Garden.
22. White Yarn House.
23. Tarring House.
24. Black Yarn House.
25. Hemp House No. 4.
26. Slopping House.
27. White House.
28. Saw Pits.
29. Capstan House.
30. Coal Yard.
31. Store of old iron.
32. Anchor Stock Shed.
33. Saw Pits.

No. 4 Building slip

(a) 14ft. 1ins.; (b) 5ft. 9ins.; (c) 155ft. 7ins.;
(d) 162ft. 1ins.; (e) 57ft. 6ins.; (f) 47ft. 0ins.

No. 5 Building slip

(a) 15ft. 6ins.; (b) 4ft. 9ins.; (c) 174ft. 9ins.;
(d) 183ft. 0ins.; (e) 56ft. 0ins.,; (f) 43ft. 9ins.

It also states that the Docks and Slips permanently covered are North Dock, Head Dock, South Dock and Nos. 1, 2, 3, 4 and 5 Building Slips.

SEA WALL

The riverside edge of the Yard, from North Corner to the Graving Slip, terminated in jetties — platforms projecting from the harbour wall supported upon piles driven deep into the mud. Several attempts had been made to build a more substantial wall, but none proved satisfactory until a sea wall designed by Mr. Rennie was undertaken.

Work commenced on 5 October, 1816, by clearing away the old foundations and piles from earlier attempts. Four rows of principal piles, 50-60 feet in length, were driven with one row of sheeting piles in front of them. Each pile, with an inclination towards the land of 4" in the foot, was driven by the dropping of a 14cwt. iron block on to it. The soil was excavated from between the piles and the space filled with limestone and gravel, rattled down solid. Sills, about 12" square and 25-30 feet long, were secured to each row of piles and the spaces between sills filled with stone. The whole area was then covered with planks 6" thick and 10 feet long.

On 1 January, 1819, the first stone of the wall — a block of Dartmoor granite 10ft. x 3ft. x 1ft. 7ins. — was laid 25 feet below the surface by Mr. Smith, Clerk of Works, who to do so, had descended in a diving bell. Captain Simeon was due to lay the stone but was indisposed. By the following New Year's Day over 40,000 cu.ft. of Dartmoor granite, much of it in blocks exceeding 4 tons in weight, had been laid.

Much of the foundation work was carried out with the help of the diving bell. Made of cast iron, it weighed 4 tons 2 cwt. and measured 6 feet long, 4 feet broad and 5 feet high. To admit light it had 12 convex lenses on top, each 8" in diameter. In the top centre there was a hole for the admission of air, connected to the surface by a leather hose. Just a short piece of leather inside acted as a non-return valve.

During the progress of construction of the sea-wall, the Duke of Gloucester on a visit to the Yard in October, 1817, descended in the bell for fifteen minutes, attended by Mr. J. Johns, Superintendent of the Works. Archduke Maximilian of Austria also visited the project and spent three-quarters of an hour in the bell below the surface.

When completed, the front of the sea-wall formed the segment of a circle with a radius of 126 feet.

A SHIP BUILT IN DOCK

In November, 1822, as all the building slips in the Yard were occupied, the keel of the "Proserpine", a 46 guns fifth rate, was laid down in the South Dock. She was floated out on 1 December, 1830. The "Proserpine" was never put in commission and remained at Devonport until 1864 when on the 21 January that year, the local naval authorities reported to the Admiralty that she had been sold to a Mr. Robinson Ridley for £2,460.

EMPLOYMENT OF CONVICTS

In June, 1826, a shipload of convicts arrived in the "Captivity" to be employed in the Yard as labourers. Within twelve months nearly 400 of them were so employed. The "Captivity" was originally the "Bellerophon" — the ship which caused such great excitement when she arrived in Plymouth Sound in 1815 with the defeated Napoleon on board.

He had made a desperate attempt to escape to America, but when he was held up at Rochefort, he surrendered to the Captain of the "Bellerophon", Frederick Lewis Maitland. The ship made for Torquay but about ten days later sailed for Plymouth. As she lay in the Sound — from 26 July to 4 August — dozens of boats milled around her with passengers trying to get a glimpse of Napoleon. The "Bellerophon" sailed with him on board, but once in the Channel, he was transferred to the "Northumberland" for his voyage to exile in St. Helena.

Later the "Bellerophon" was converted to a Prison Ship; was re-named "Captivity" in October, 1824 and she served in that capacity at Plymouth from 1826 to 1836.

H.M.S. Captivity alongside the Dockyard

CHANGES IN ADMINISTRATION

An important change in the Yard's administration took place in 1832. The establishment had outgrown the system of supervision represented by a Commissioner and his Senior Officers. Circumstances demanded a change, so that year an edict went forth to abolish the office of Commissioner and to revise the list of officials. Ever since 1691 the command had been vested in Captains, R.N., and the difficulties which they frequently encountered made the appointment anything but an enviable one.

By an Order-in-Council dated 27 June, 1832, the new office of Superintendent was instituted and Plymouth Yard was honoured by being made a Flag Officer's appointment carrying with it greater prestige and importance. The first officer to hold the appointment was Rear Admiral Frederic Warren who joined the Dockyard on 1 April, 1837.

DOCKYARD POLICE FORCE FORMED

In 1829 Sir Robert Peel had formed the first Police Force in England — the Metropolitan Police. Four years later the Admiralty introduced a Dockyard Police Force, although they were not used at Plymouth Yard until 20 May, 1834. The new force was formed by remodelling the existing collection of Warders and Watchmen. For the first time, uniforms were worn — stove-pipe hats and a silver-buttoned blue frock coat cut away at the front from the waist downwards. Their trousers were of white duck in the summer, but darker in the winter. They still carried rattles to raise any alarm, but they also carried truncheons ornately decorated with the Sovereign's Coat of Arms and the man's number.

The policemen on joining were given a complete issue of uniform but on leaving the Force deductions were made from their final payments for any items not returned. In addition, to quote the regulations, "the sum of five shillings shall be retained to pay for altering his clothing to fit his successor."

These Dockyard policemen received "good wages" — 19/- for a seven day week — and various incentive schemes. A reward of £2.10s.0d. was given to policemen "who detected persons embezzling Government stores after such persons had been found guilty in a summary court; and a reward of up to £10 in cases where offenders were convicted on indictment."

NORTH DOCK

In 1839, a contract was signed with Mr. T. Elwill to carry out various alterations and additions to the dry docks. These included the lengthening and widening of North Dock, and enlarging its gates. Originally 56ft. 2ins. wide, the entrance was increased to 64 feet, and the dock made 20 feet longer. The work was completed at Christmas, 1839.

DOCKYARD BATTALIONS

In the 1840's Dockyard Battalions of adult employees were formed for the protection of the Dockyard ports. A wide variety of military service were performed by these Battalions, each of which being divided into Artillery, Sappers, Infantry, Boat and Recruit sections. Each also had its own band.

The Battalions were of considerable numerical strength — that at Devonport in 1853 totalling 1,598, with representatives of every trade amongst the other ranks, and officered by the Principal and Subordinate Officers of the various departments. A Royal Marine officer was Adjutant and was responsible for the efficiency of the Battalion in drill and equipment. The other ranks were paid 1/- per night for drilling, which was done after working hours under the direction of retired Royal Marine instructors, and each man was loaned a complete kit free of charge.

CHAPTER 7

TEN YEARS WASTED LABOUR

About 1838, a proposal was made to the Admiralty to rebuild the walls of No. 1 Basin, the work being placed in the charge of Mr. Taylor, Civil Architect of the Navy. When about £3,000 had been spent on the work, by which time Mr. Taylor had retired, Colonel Brandreth of the Royal Engineers was appointed to superintend the engineering works of the Royal Dockyards. Thereupon, a much larger, more comprehensive scheme for improving the capabilities of the Yard was proposed.

The necessary plans were drawn up by Mr. T.J. Hawkes, the Master Shipwright in Plymouth Yard. Not one of the other Dockyard officers raised any objection. On the contrary, the proposed measures received every encouragement — so the work was put in hand.

In consideration of the enlarged dimensions of ships and the great need of dock accommodation in the Yard, it was planned to construct a large closed basin within which four or five sail of the line could be easily and expeditiously fitted out, and with the required storehouses situated close at hand. From this basin would lead two large docks capable of receiving the largest ships in the Navy, fully stored and with the advantage of allowing the docking procedure twice every 24 hours and whenever most convenient.

This plan was to be implemented by the conversion of No. 1 Basin and Dock, and the adjacent Double Dock which was then greatly in need of repair and, for the refit of which, a large sum of money would be required. At the same time, the boundary wall of the Dockyard was to be extended northwards across Cornwall Street to join up with the wall of the Gun Wharf (P.R.O. Adm. 140/168 dated 28 December, 1840). Within this area, it was proposed to build another dock capable of taking a ship of the largest class. It also entailed taking in the public area at North Corner, where another basin for keeping boats or for the landing of timber was to be made.

A new slip was proposed across No. 5 building slip at Mutton Cove, with a plan to extend the Yard southwards to incorporate an area covered by some of the houses bordering the small harbour at Mutton Cove.

When about ten years labour — overcoming considerable engineering difficulties — and £100,000 had been expended in building dams and sea walls, and with the great project nearing completion, Colonel Brandreth left his department to be succeeded by another military engineer, Colonel Irvine.

At this critical juncture, the then Master Shipwright of the Yard, W. Edye, persuaded the Admiralty that the whole plan was a blunder. They thereupon decided that the scheme should be cast aside.

In consequence of strong representations about their inefficiency and extravagance, the Admiralty — not appearing to have any confidence in their own officers — called in Mr. Rendel, a Civil Engineer engaged in private practice, and sent him to Devonport to inspect the state of the Yard and report thereon. After an expensive and laborious investigation, he told the Admiralty that the scheme then being carried out was extravagant and impracticable. To reduce expenditure, he suggested that the easiest way out would be to get rid of these new docks, reduce the size of the basin, but extend the jetties.

The excavation for one of the docks, although far advanced, was accordingly filled in and Mr. Rendel's suggestions ordered to be put into effect.

After a short time though, work was stopped. In February, 1850, Mr. Rendel was again sent to Devonport along with two other engineers, Messrs. Walker and Cubitt, and some members of the Board of Admiralty, to make a further report on his own plan. This visit resulted in a proposal for two docks but with a smaller basin. However, this was not approved by the full Board and for a while all work was suspended.

Mr. W. Churchward, who had long been employed on the works, then offered the Board a plan by which a part of the Double Dock was to be saved and two large docks still built into the basin. The proposal though was not entertained by the Board; probably out of compliment to their own engineers.

The final plan was submitted by Colonel Green, Director of Works, whereby one dock only was to be completed, but judiciously, he managed to leave the overall problem open to allow any future return to the original plan.

Successive Boards of Admiralty had passed through a series of varying evolutions but had returned to the same point from which they had started — a pretty expensive policy but one which had done nothing to improve the capabilities of the Yard.

Work proceeded only on the original No. 1 Dock and Basin, the Dock being made large enough to take a first rate with all her guns and stores on board. In 1853 the Basin was deepened and part of the north angle of the surrounding wall taken down to make the entrance wide enough to admit the class of ships then being built.

When work was completed in 1854, the first ship into the reconstructed No. 1 Dock was "Exmouth" to have her bottom coppered.

THE DOCKYARD'S GREATEST FIRE

Sunday, 27 September, 1840 was a memorable day in the history of Plymouth Dockyard. In those days there was no early closing of the Yard on a Saturday, and when the workmen left on the evening of the 26th everything seemed to be in order. At 6 p.m. a report that "all was safe" was made by Mr. Spiers, Carpenter of the 74 guns "Talavera". This ship, which was lying in Head Dock, had been laid down at Woolwich Dockyard as the "Thunderer" but was re-named "Talavera" in July, 1817 before being launched on 15 October, 1818.

The Captain of the Guard made his rounds at 3 a.m. on the 27th and still nothing appeared amiss. At 4.15 a.m. though a Police Officer on duty suddenly observed smoke issuing from the bow portholes of the "Talavera", and the alarm was raised. The fire-fighting resources of the Yard were quite inadequate to cope with the fire but soon men of the 11th, 53rd, and 65th Regiments of the Royal Artillery, and the Royal Marines, with their engines, appeared. The Devonport Town engine and the West of England Insurance Company's engine from Plymouth also attended. At that time there were also floating engines in the "Ordinary" and these were brought to take up position outside the dock. In all there were 36 engines — manuals, of course — but they were practically powerless to cope with the raging inferno.

In 17 minutes from the discovery of the smoke by the policeman, the "Talavera", some dockside sheds and a large quantity of timber stacked along

The Great Fire of 1840

the wharves, were one entire mass of flame. In the Stern Dock to the rear of that in which the "Talavera" lay, was the "Minden", another 74 guns ship launched in Bombay Dockyard on 19 June, 1810. Parallel to the Head and Stern Docks was South (No. 1) Dock in which the 28 guns sixth rate "Imogene" was lying. The fire spread to the roof erected over the South Dock and by 5.15 a.m. both the ship and the roof were a mass of flame. Great efforts were made to prevent the fire, which had caught the bowsprit and figurehead of the "Minden", from destroying that ship. Although the order was given to the ship's company to abandon ship, they stuck to their task and saved her. Courageous work was done by some Dockyard shipwrights who threw baulks of timber into the dock and standing on them, beside the burning ship, cut large holes in the hull which enabled the rising tide to enter and scuttle the ship and help put out the fire.

The "Imogene", launched at Pembroke Dock on 24 June, 1831, and the "Talavera" were both destroyed, but the "Minden" survived the fire to be converted to a Hospital Ship in April, 1842.

Great fears were entertained for the Rigging House, which, if set alight, might then have involved the whole Yard, but the spread of the fire in that direction was prevented.

Amongst the buildings on the dockside to be destroyed though, was the Adelaide Gallery. This building, named after Queen Adelaide, was a great feature to all visitors to the establishment. It had been erected in 1826 as a shipwrights' shop, but Captain C.B.H. Ross, C.B., Superintendent of the Yard, set it aside as a Museum for housing a fine collection of ships' figureheads and similar trophies of the Navy. In the Gallery was a sphinx brought home in the "Talavera", and intended for the British Museum. This memorial, which had recently been rescued from the sands of Egypt and reported to be 3,000 years old, was destroyed in the fire.

Most of the ships' figureheads were destroyed, also the flag that floated over Nelson and under which he fell at Trafalgar; and Lord Exmouth's flag at the taking of Algiers. The irony of fate was exemplified in the destruction of the capstan of the "Royal George" which had been submerged since the ship foundered at Spithead in August, 1782. After its recovery, it was deposited in the Adelaide Gallery — only to be destroyed by fire.

There was talk at the time that the fire was due to arson, and some of the circumstances seemed to point that way, but nothing of the kind was ever proved.

NAME CHANGED TO DEVONPORT DOCKYARD

Although the name of the town surrounding the Yard had been changed — Plymouth Dock had become Devonport on 1 January, 1824 — the Dockyard retained the name Plymouth Yard until August, 1843. Then, during a visit to the Yard by H.M. Queen Victoria and the Prince Consort, she gave approval to the name being changed to Devonport Yard.

During this visit, the Royal couple visited and inspected the "Hindostan". Teak built, her timbers had been converted in India and sent home. She was laid down in a covered slipway in the Yard in August, 1828, but was not launched until thirteen years later — 2 August, 1841. For twenty years she lay idle in the Hamoaze, until, at the end of 1865, she was taken to Dartmouth to form part of the "Britannia", the Cadets' Training School. In 1905 she was towed to Portsmouth where she formed part of "Fisgard" until being broken up in 1921.

A DOCKYARD SCHOOL FORMED

A school for Dockyard apprentices was approved by an Order in Council dated 1 February, 1843 and was opened in 1844 in a building at the head of South (No. 1) Dock, the Master being one of the accountant clerks of the Yard. The school was transferred about 1850 to a site on what had formerly been the officers' stables.

A copy of the first time-table of the school, dated June, 1844, and signed by Samuel Pym, (Admiral Superintendent 1841-46), reveals what a remarkably different opinion was held then as to the educational needs of Dockyard apprentices. For example, time was allocated almost every day to prayer and catechism, religious exercises, and — weekly — an examination by the Chaplain. The very different facilities for education then existing in the town is borne out by a report on Dockyard schools dated 1857, which pointed out that only at Pembroke Dock did entrants to the Dockyard conform with the condition requiring a competent knowledge of reading, writing and arithmetic. Some of the apprentices failed on all these counts!

SHOALING

In the late 1840's there were two classes of shipwrights, one of which received a higher rate of pay in consideration of length of service, ability and the special nature of the work on which they were employed.

After much agitation against this system of classification, the men receiving the lower rate of pay had their pay increased to the higher rate, which then became the uniform wage for shipwrights throughout the Yard.

There then developed at Devonport a very objectionable practice of reserving the best shipwrights in the Yard, forming them into four gangs, and afterwards leaving the rest of the men to be "shoaled". This meant that the weakest and most infirm men were often sent afloat, even out into the Sound, while the strongest and best men were employed upon a particular ship with the view of speeding up her construction and making her appear cheap through having so much less labour charged to her.

In 1849 it was recommended that the practice should be discontinued and that future "shoaling" should be general, so that each gang in the Yard should be of equal strength, as is done at all other Yards. (Admiralty Board Minute No. 5, dated 25 January, 1849).

The system still continued to have its critics. The Senior Foreman of the Yard had first choice of six men, and the others made their choice in order of seniority. Although the gangs of shipwrights were supposed to be selected with due regard to their ability, each Foreman obviously tried to get the best men. However, the system of "shoaling" enabled officials to get rid of any member of their gang with whom they were unable to work in harmony; whilst the men themselves had the privilege of being transferred to another gang if they so desired.

CHANGES IN THE METHOD OF MUSTER

On 1 April, 1849, it was decided to adopt the Chatham system of muster by tickets. Provision was made in the annual estimates for the erection at Devonport of the necessary buildings for housing ticket tables. Tickets were to be taken up by the men from these "muster galleries", deposited in boxes and kept at their place of work by Leading Men and Heads of Trade to which the men belonged. Boxes were not to be re-opened until the 'ten minutes bell' for dinner or leaving the Yard at the end of the day had actually begun to ring. Muster galleries were opened at the same time, and not before, so that the men having taken up their tickets at the ship's side could deposit them in the muster gallery, yet not leave the Yard before time.

RE-NUMBERING THE BUILDING SLIPS

In 1849, the Building Slips were re-numbered with the southernmost one at Mutton Cove becoming No. 1. Hitherto they had been numbered from North to South, even, at one period, including the Graving Slip north of the Camber as No. 1 (P.R.O. Adm. 140/170 dated 18 June, 1849). For most of the years though, since the slips at Mutton Cove had been built, the Graving Slip had not been numbered, and the remainder were numbered 1 to 5.

The significance of this year of change should be borne in mind when noting from which slips various ships had been launched. For instance, the first rate "Britannia" was laid down on No. 1 slip and the "Conqueror" on No. 5. However, this was the same slip, the "Britannia" having been laid down on it in 1813 and "Conqueror", after the slip had been re-numbered, in 1853.

CHAPTER 8

THE ADVENT OF STEAM

The 1820's saw the advent of steam propulsion into the Royal Navy. The first vessels to be fitted were little more than despatch vessels or tugs, although one of the most successful ships was H.M.S. Lightning, a wooden paddle wheel gun vessel launched at Deptford Yard on 19 September, 1823.

The first steam fighting ship built by the Admiralty at the Plymouth Yard was the "Rhadamanthus". A steam paddle vessel, 813 tons burthen, designed by the local Master Shipwright, Thomas Roberts, she was laid down during September, 1831 in dock, and not on a slipway. In the presence of a large crowd, she was floated out of the dock during the afternoon of Monday, 16 April, 1832. However, her engines were not built or fitted locally. Ten days after being put afloat, she sailed under jury-rig for Woolwich, where she was fitted with engines made by Maudsley Sons and Field.

The question of the suitability of screw propellers in lieu of paddle wheels received much attention in the Admiralty. The principle of the propeller had been known for some time but it was from the result of a series of actual experiments that it was decided that the screw was more suitable than paddle wheels for most vessels.

In 1848 though the Royal Navy did not possess a single line-of-battle ship propelled by a screw. One block ship completed and two others in preparation were, at that time, the only British vessels of that type to which a screw had been fitted.

Up to the year 1850, notwithstanding the progress made in adapting screw propulsion to the mercantile navy, and some very striking results obtained by some small vessels fitted with screws belonging to the Royal Navy, the Admiralty were slow and cautious in accepting this new power throughout the fleet.

At the close of 1852, the "Agamemnon", 91 guns, had been launched, commissioned and tried at sea. She was the first steam line-of-battle ship, designed as such and produced by one of Her Majesty's Dockyards — Woolwich.

A few months previously, the "Sans Pareil", 70 guns, had been launched from No. 5 slip at Devonport after being altered and fitted for a screw. She was lengthened aft by about seven feet to give her a finer run for the screw propeller, and lengthened at the fore foot to make the stem more perpendicular in order to give a sharper entrance into the water. However, the results in "Sans Pareil" were not entirely satisfactory. Nevertheless, the ice was broken — the "Agamemnon" was perfectly successful, so the power of the screw was established and the days of sailing vessels as instruments of war were clearly numbered.

SHIP CONVERSIONS

In 1850 Great Britain possessed 86 line-of-battle ships, all sailing vessels — many of them over thirty years old — besides 104 frigates of all classes. Could these ships be adapted to the new power or was a new navy to be built? These questions received an answer from subsequent events. In 1854 war was declared, by which time just three line-of-battle screw ships had been designed, built and sent to sea — "Agamemnon", 91 guns, "James Watt", 91 guns, and "St. Jean d'Acre", 101 guns. The last named, built at Devonport, was the largest two-decker then built and the largest steamship that had so far been built at Devonport — and the quickest built. She was laid down on No. 5 slip in June, 1851 and launched at 4 p.m. on Wednesday, 23 March, 1853. During her trials in September of that year, she averaged nine knots. Her propeller, weighing seven tons, could be raised and stowed when the ship was under sail.

Five other ships, whilst still on the slips, had been altered by adding to their length — including the "Algiers", 91 guns, at Devonport — and seven more prepared for the screw without any alteration other than that involved in making the aperture for the shaft. Ships altered by both methods were placed side by side on active service and comparisons between them could then easily be made. It was at once seen that the former possessed an unquestionable superiority in space, armament and speed. It proved though that converted ships, even in the simplest form of adaption to the screw, could render important services and the saving of time, money and materials in either form of conversion was immense.

A table produced in October, 1860 by Mr. B.W. Walker, Controller of the Navy, revealed that the conversion of thirty sail of the line and four large frigates was effected for little more than £1 million with about 23,500 loads of timber; whereas if similar ships had been built they would have cost nearly £3 million and would have consumed over 136,000 loads of timber. It was a matter of necessity to convert those ships in order to meet the national requirements, for even if money had been of no consideration, timber to the extent required could not easily have been procured, nor were slips available on which to build them.

Amongst the 34 ships listed in the table, the following were converted at Devonport between the dates shown:-

42

Algiers — 27 September, 1852 - 26 January, 1854; **Nile** — 6 December, 1852 - 30 January, 1854; **Exmouth** — 20 June, 1853 - 12 July, 1854; **Centurion** — 28 September,1854 - 12 November, 1855; **Aboukir** — 8 October, 1856 - 1 January, 1858; **London** — January 1857 - 13 May, 1858; **Lion** — 1 February, 1858 - 17 May, 1859; **St. George** — 21 August, 1858- 19 March, 1859; **Royal William** — 21 March, 1859 - 9 February, 1860; **Phoebe** — 20 May, 1859 - 10 April, 1860.

Conversions often necessitated the ship being lengthened by "cutting asunder" — cutting the ship in half — separating the two parts and adding in a new section. To the after body was fitted a cradle as for launching, with bilge ways, poppets, etc. The shores were then removed from the after body and with the assistance of blocks and wedges it was slid apart the required extent.

FORMATION OF THE STEAM YARD

As the adoption of steam propulsion for naval ships became more general it was obvious that it would be necessary to provide a separate establishment in each of the Royal Dockyards which could deal with all the normal repairs and replacements that might be required for these steam ships. The lack of such an engineering establishment at Devonport frequently involved considerable delay by ships having to be sent to Portsmouth or Woolwich.

Furthermore, the existing wharfage accommodation in Devonport Yard was extremely limited, and with the increasing dimensions of fighting ships it was also imperative to provide larger graving docks which could also be entered at any state of the tide. At this time there was not a dock at Devonport capable of taking the larger men-of-war. This fact was proved when an attempt was made to dock the second rate, 90 guns, "Albion". After removing her chain cable and a great deal of ballast she still could not be docked for want of water.

After a careful survey had been made on both sides of the River Tamar, a site half a mile upstream from the original Dockyard establishment was chosen. Accordingly, 38 acres of land, together with 43 acres of foreshore, were purchased from the Trustees of the will of Sir. I. St. Aubyn.

The general lay-out of the proposed development was thus described by Sir John Rennie:-

"Here it is proposed to construct two floating basins about six acres each, with entrances 80 feet wide, laid at a depth sufficient for the largest steamer to enter and depart at all times of the tide; there are to be three large docks besides the lock, which is to be constructed as to answer the purpose of a dock when required. There are to be complete engine and boiler workshops, with the requisite tools and store-houses for fitting-out and repairing large fleets of steamers; the whole establishment will cover a surface of about 72 acres."

The contractors appointed were Messrs. George Baker and Sons, who in the first place excavated the docks and basins whilst work on the associated buildings commenced two years later.

The foundation of Keyham Yard, as it was to become known, was commemorated on 12 September, 1846, when the Rt. Hon. the Earl of Auckland, G.C.B., then First Lord of the Admiralty, laid a huge nine tons block of granite in which had been placed a box containing all the current coins of the realm. This block was incorporated into the South Lock entrance to the basin.

About three years later, in May, 1849, questions were being asked in Parliament about the cost and extravagance of the new works at Keyham. When first proposed, Parliament had been informed that the work would cost about £400,000. On 25 September, 1844 Mr. Baker, the contractor, had proposed to the Admiralty a plan of operations which required £713,000. In 1848 the estimate had increased to £1,225,000 and the following year to £1,322,627. It was evident that between 1844 and 1848 Parliament had been very much misinformed with regard to the overall cost of these works. In fact, if they had known just what these works were really going to cost they might not have approved the scheme; but they had, and by then work was well in hand.

An extensive cofferdam, 1,600 feet long and 26 feet wide, was built on a north - south line on the river side of the site to cut off the area from the tide and to enable it to be pumped dry. In October, 1844, three Devonport built ships — "Saracen", "Scorpion" and "Lyra" — were appropriated to provide additional protection.

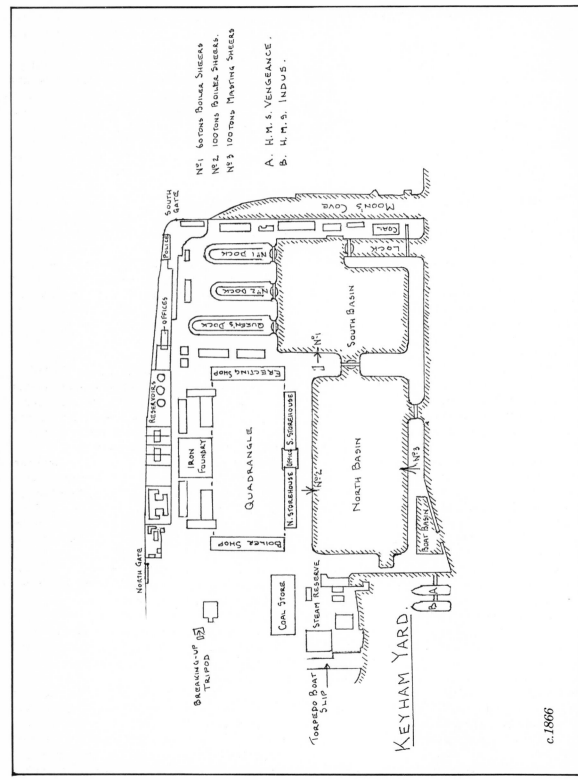

KEYHAM YARD.

c. 1866

No.1 60 TONS BOILER SHEERS
No.2 100 TONS BOILER SHEERS.
No.3 100 TONS MASTING SHEERS

A. H.M.S. VENGEANCE.
B. H.M.S. INDUS.

NORTH GATE

BREAKING-UP
TRIPOD

COAL STORE

STEAM RESERVE

TORPEDO BOAT
SLIP

RESERVOIRS

IRON
FOUNDRY

QUADRANGLE

BOILER SHOP

ERECTING SHOP

N. STOREHOUSE
OFFICE S. STOREHOUSE

OFFICES

POLICE

SOUTH GATE

No.1 DOCK

No.2 DOCK

QUEEN'S DOCK

No.1

No.2

No.3

NORTH BASIN

SOUTH BASIN

BOAT BASIN

LOCK

COAL

Moon's Cove

A
B

It was a great day for James Nasmyth when his four tons steam hammer, with blows delivered at the rate of 80 per minute, drove the first pile in the construction of the protecting cofferdam. It was sunk to the required depth in 4½ minutes compared with more than twelve hours needed to drive a similar pile working by the old method of "tilt" hammers. Only a year or so before, the Admiralty had ordered one of Nasmyth's steam hammers, then recently patented, to be erected in the Smithery in Devonport Yard. At that time the heavier forgings were being treated by the "Hercules" — a mass of iron weighing between six and eight hundredweight which used to be hauled up by means of ropes and pullies to a height of about eight feet and the ropes let go, the mass falling on the pre-heated forging.

The surplus material excavated from the site within the cofferdam was taken northwards and dumped in Keyham Creek and Lake. Mud dredged from in front of the Yard was deposited in deep holes near Drake's Island.

The selected area was separated from the original Yard by War Office and local Corporation property, and the northern limit of the proposed Steam Yard adjoined the Ordnance Department's Keyham Depot. The Basin could not be completed until alternative accommodation for that Department's powder magazine had been provided at Bull Point, about two miles further up the river. Bull Point was purchased from Thomas Elliot on 8 November, 1845, and additional land adjoining, from Charles Trelawney on 8 July, 1846. The greater part of this area was transferred to the Ordnance Department in exchange for their Depot at Keyham Point on 10 February, 1847. On 1 October, 1891 it became Admiralty property as the Naval Ordnance Depot.

The eastern boundary of the Steam Yard — the limit of the excavation made in the shillet rock — was a great wall running from north to south. Inside this wall were built the offices used by the various departments, but which were replaced by more extensive buildings in 1911.

The two basins at Keyham were originally known as the South and North Basins, later to become Nos. 2 and 3 respectively — and the entrance was South Lock.

The Lock and Docks were drained by a steam-driven pumping installation constructed on the south side of No. 2 Basin. By 1850 that Basin and the entrance Lock had been completed. Water was let into the Lock for the first time on Saturday 4 May, 1850, but it was not let into the Docks and Basins though until May, 1853. Twenty four hours afterwards the three caissons, built by Messrs. Grissell of London, were floated into place.

The Steam Yard was officially opened on 7 October, 1853, when H.M.S. Queen with her ship's company manning the yards, was taken into the basin.

Although only a short distance from the Dockyard, the Steam Yard operated as an entirely separate Yard — different hours of work, rates of pay and conditions. In 1853 even a separate Police Force, comprising an Inspector and twelve Police Constables, was sent from the Dockyard to do duty at Keyham. It was not until 1876 that the Steam Yard became fully integrated with the rest of the Yard.

THE QUADRANGLE

With the building of Keyham Yard, the hub of the Engineering Department was established at the Quadrangle, an area of about six acres under one glass roof, which was also colloquially known as The Factory. It was designed by Charles Barry, architect of the Houses of Parliament.

The workshops were on three sides of an open space about 780ft. x 350ft., the west side adjacent to No. 3 Basin having North and South Store rooms straddling an office block. On the northern side of it were the Boiler Shop, Boilersmiths' Shop and Platers' Shop; on the east, the Iron Foundry, Millwrights' and Pattern Shop, and Brass Foundry; whilst to the south were the Coppersmiths' and Blacksmiths' Shops with the Fitting and Erecting Shops behind.

Amongst the first buildings completed — below ground level — were cells for the prisoners who were employed on the heavy work; followed soon afterwards by above ground accommodation for their warders.

A small Fitting Shop north of the Foundry on the east side of the Quadrangle was opened in 1855 and appears to have been the first workshop specifically built for the Engineering Department.

Apart from direct production shops, provision was also made for supporting facilities; a Leather

North Basin at Keyham

South Basin at Keyham

Shop for maintaining driving belts and preparing plunger washers for hydraulic pumps which were important for heavy gun mountings; a Bottle Test Shop for testing containers and reservoirs for compressed air or gases; a Lagging Shop and even a Laundry for washing the men's overalls.

COAL DEPOT AT KEYHAM

Near the Lock entrance into No. 2 Basin at Keyham, a new Coal Depot was completed in 1860. Designed in the office of the Director of Works, London, the first of its kind was built at Woolwich. An officer from Keyham was then sent to acquaint himself with the particulars for adapting one to the site at Keyham. Built at a cost of £7,000 it was intended to contain 5,000 tons of coal and to supersede manual labour. Coal was lifted from coal ships by steam elevator direct into store and it passed out from the top of the store down on to a weighing machine. From there through several chutes, the coal passed into sacks then on to carts for transfer to wherever a ship needed coal. Vessels could not coal direct from the Depot, but were usually berthed in the Basin.

However, after just a few years the system fell into disuse. It was feared that the great weight — coal and machinery — would have caused it to collapse into the creek. Coal was then manhandled until a hydraulic system was installed.

TUNNEL CONNECTING THE TWO YARDS

On 2 June, 1854 Parliament passed an Act "to empower the Commissioners of the Admiralty to construct a tunnel between H.M. Dockyard at Devonport and H.M. Steam Yard at Keyham, and to acquire certain property for H.M. Service to make and construct the tunnel or partly by a tunnel and partly by open cutting; and to lay down and work a railway in said tunnel."

Plans for the 946 yards long tunnel were drawn by a Mr. Damant and the contractors for the operations were Messrs. Smith of Woolwich, who were also contractors for new docks at Portsmouth Dockyard and Pembroke Dock. Superintendent of the work was Mr. J. MacDonnell who in November, 1856 was succeeded by Mr. Hoppen.

The tunnel made communication between the two Yards independent of the intervening Corporation property and enabled rail communication to be made to the Dockyard from the main line system.

Work commenced in April, 1855 with about 270 men being employed on excavations at nine different points along the line. A temporary tramway was led from the southern entrance of the tunnel to North Jetty for transporting excavated material to barges for deposit on to the left bank of Millbrook Lake, near Anderton.

The tunnel was completed in May, 1857, although foot traffic had been able to use it for a month previously. In the early years, during times of high rainfall, the tunnel would be flooded by water percolating through the ground, sometimes to a depth of 12" - 15" until the tide receded. All traffic between the Yards had to be effected by horse and cart. However, at the beginning of 1879 the tunnel was closed for a month, during which time a narrow gauge railway was laid upon a bed of concrete; and a raised footpath constructed. The rails were subsequently extended to the extreme end of the Yard, and stores were conveyed between the two Yards pulled by a light locomotive.

The railway line, on emerging from the southern end of the tunnel, passed through the North Smithery, causing the loss of a blast furnace. The Admiralty thereupon sanctioned that the saw pits in front of the building slips be filled in and another blast furnace built there as an extension to the South Smithery.

At right angles with the tunnel as it emerged into the Dockyard was a narrow tram-road which, with an exceedingly steep rising gradient of 1 in 5, led to the main gate. At the top was fixed a 30 h.p. steam engine and double action crane. Costing £2,000 to construct, it was fixed by order of Rear Admiral the Hon. J.R. Drummond when he was the Admiral Superintendent (1866-70) for the purpose of hauling up and lowering down carts and wagons of various kinds that had occasion to enter or leave the Yard. These carts passing along the main road within sight and sound of the Admiral's official residence, proved objectionable to his wife so the tram-road was put out of action and allowed to fall into disuse. Mrs. Drummond also found the quarter-hour chimes of the Dockyard clock annoying, so she had them stopped, too!

ALTERATIONS IN KEYHAM STEAM YARD

The principle alterations made to the docks at Keyham after they were first built were

(a) the lengthening at the head of No. 1 dock to receive the troopship "Himalaya".

(b) recessing the lower altars of No. 2 dock to allow the paddle wheels of certain vessels to be kept in place when those vessels were docked; and

(c) lengthening of No. 3 or Queen's dock by over 100 feet to allow the longer vessels such as the armoured ship "Warrior" to be docked.

However, the extra draught of "Warrior" would have prevented her entering No. 3 dock but for an ingenious method of overcoming such a handicap. The sill of the inner end of the entrance lock was only 28 feet deep so this was lowered by nine feet. This deepening was then carried into the basin by a "canal" — a channel leading to the entrance of No. 3 dock. The need to have to do this highlighted the shortcomings in the design of having the largest dock (No. 3) not in a straight line with the entrance. Amazingly whilst the excavation of this canal across the bottom of South Basin was in progress, it did not prevent the use of the other two docks. The basin was flooded to allow docking of ships and then pumped out again to continue the work.

DOCK ACCOMMODATION AT DEVONPORT

A Select Committee appointed to inquire into, and report upon, the basin and dock accommodation of the Dockyards, made the following remarks in their report published at the end of August, 1864:-

"The unanimous opinion of the witnesses, naval and civil, who have had the advantage of practical experience at Devonport, including three officers, of whom two have held, and the third now holds, the appointment of Admiral Superintendent, is that the dock and quay accommodation at that port is insufficient, and the Controller of the Navy and the Director of Works concur in this opinion. Some of these witnesses think that two additional first class docks are required; others, that three would be absolutely necessary. All agree as to the necessity of additional quay accommodation and, with the exception of the present Admiral

Superintendent, that it "should be obtained by the construction of a third basin at Keyham. In order, however, to avoid expense, Admiral Symonds suggests that sufficient accommodation might be provided by means of wharves carried out from the sea wall of the Keyham basins into deep water, where ships could lie alongside in the stream; but the Director of Works, and the local Superintending Civil Engineer, object to this arrangement, the latter on account of the great distance from the sea wall to deep water, which is 700 feet, and the danger which would result of 'silting up the lock entrance to the basins, if this space were occupied by jetties. In addition to this objection the engineering evidence shows that wharfage so obtained would not be of the same value as in a basin."

"The Factory is not worked at present to nearly its full extent; but it appears from the evidence of Mr. Lloyd, the Engineer-in-Chief of the Navy, and of Mr. Miller, the Chief Engineer on the spot, that the existing docks and basins are insufficient for the work at present being done at Keyham; and it is estimated by the former that the quantity of work will be nearly doubled when the engines of the several powerful steamships of between 50,000 and 60,000 horse power, which have been built within the last six or seven years, shall come, for the first time, under extensive repair. Even now the want of dock and basin accommodation leads to delay, unnecessary expense, and inferior workmanship; and your Committee are of opinion that a third basin at Devonport, equal in extent to the present north basin, and at least two additional first class docks, are among the works required; and that it is desirable that the entrance to the basin and docks be so constructed as to admit ships at all times of the tide."

It was to be several years before additional docks were to be provided, but within two years work commenced on an extension to the North Basin at Keyham. The basin as originally constructed was about 450 feet wide, from the river side to the opposite wall, and about 500 feet long, from north to south, with a depth of 34 feet. Large as this seemed, ships could only be taken in and out at spring tides; a disadvantage which was increased during the short days of the winter months when the highest tides frequently occurred after dark. The basin was extended to a length of 882 feet and deepened to 40 feet, which allowed the largest ships to be taken in or out, even at neap tides. At the north end of the extension an additional entrance was provided in anticipation that it might provide communication with any basin that in the future might be built to the northwards.

An engine house was built at the southern end of the area in which were placed engines from the wooden sloop "Desperate" — broken up at Devonport in August, 1865 — and used to drive a centrifugal pump by which the water level in the South Basin could be raised eight feet in two hours.

At the same time a railway was constructed northwards to connect Keyham Yard with the system of the Cornwall Railway. This branch formed a junction with the main line near the bridge under which the railway passed the Saltash Road just before crossing Weston Mill Creek, and at a declivity of 1 in 70 ran down to a terminus in Keyham Yard where there was a turn-table to pass the trucks or carriages on to existing lines. This line formed a portion of the scheme carried out by Mr. Drew of Burnard Place, Plymouth, which embraced the extension through the tunnel to the Dockyard.

SHIPS EXCHANGED WITH PRUSSIA

The fifth rate "Thetis" was launched at Devonport in August, 1846. When she returned in 1854, after nearly four years in the Pacific, an agreement was reached between the British and Prussian Governments to exchange the "Thetis" for two paddle-wheel iron vessels of 600 tons each. The Prussian vessels each had four mortars and two 32 pounder guns, but the "Thetis" was transferred without her armament. In October she was taken into dock at Devonport for preparation for early delivery to the Prussians, who wanted her before the ice set in around their harbours.

A NEW TYPE "FLOATING DOCK" AT KEYHAM

On 2 June, 1876, a new floating tray for the purpose of docking vessels up to 2,000 tons was to be brought in to use at Keyham, with the gunboat "Seagull" being placed upon it. This tray, or dock, was built on the Thames and towed to Devonport. It was taken in to the Lock and the water was pumped out in order that the tray might be placed properly on the blocks. When the Lock was flooded, the tray — with its valves open — should have remained on the blocks. That would have allowed the "Seagull" to be floated in and "docked" in the tray. That was the theory!! Unfortunately through the inability of the valves of the tray to admit the water as rapidly as the valves of the Lock, the tray, instead of remaining on the bottom, floated. However, after further trials the problem was overcome and the "floating tray" was brought into general use. With a ship docked therein the tray could be moved to any part of the yard to allow underwater work to be carried out on the ship. It proved a cheaper method than the usual docking procedure and also eased the pressure on the other docks.

PROGRESS OF ENGINEERING

The progress of engineering in the Royal Navy, the increase in the number of ships and the dimensions of the machinery being put in them, brought increased demands upon the Factory at Keyham. The refits of such important vessels as the battleships "Lord Clyde" and "Lord Warden" were undertaken with great success. As an example of the scope of the work undertaken, in 1869 new cylinders were cast, machined and fitted to the "Lord Clyde", and as these cylinders were no less than 10 feet in diameter and 45 tons in weight, it will be recognised as an engineering feat of considerable magnitude. The Yard gave notice that the pubic would be admitted to the Foundry to witness the actual casting being done, and a large number availed themselves of the opportunity. On Saturday, 27 November 1869, work commenced at 4 a.m.; between 10 and 11 a.m. moulten metal began to be loaded into cauldrons and at noon pouring into the mould commenced.

However, machinery for newly built ships continued to be manufactured by various contractors, even though difficulties frequently occurred. The torpedo-gunboat "Sandfly", laid down at Devonport on 19 April 1886, would normally have expected to have been launched within twelve months but she was on the slipway for more than seventeen months because of the delay by the Admiralty in placing the contract for her machinery. When the "Pelican" — a sloop laid down at Devonport in March, 1875 — was nearly ready for launch, it was discovered that insufficient space had been allotted for her machinery. Then, pending alterations of the hull space, complications arose with the firm holding the contract to supply her engines. Her original machinery had been designed by the Yorkshire Engine Company under letters patent granted to a Mr. Loftus Perkins, an enterprising American who also had an establishment in London. Disagreement arose between the manufacturers of the machinery and Mr. Perkins which prevented the engines intended for the "Pelican" from being completed. The parts which had already been made were broken up. She was subsequently fitted with the engines, made by Messrs. Humphrys, Tennant and Company of Deptford, which had been intended for her sister ship "Cormorant" then building at Chatham.

The first ship's engines made in the Yard at Keyham — whose officials had competed against private firms for the contract — were for the composite single screw first class gunboats "Pheasant" and "Partridge". Both were laid down on 6 June, 1877, the "Pheasant" being launched on 10 April, 1888 and the "Partridge" exactly one month later.

CHAPTER 9

DOCKYARD GATES

The Keyham establishment, at its southern end, had an imposing entrance which was based on a design produced by Mr. William Scamp of the Admiralty Department of Works. A model of his design still survives in the Dockyard Museum. This Albert Road gate, as it became known, was closed for the last time on 4 September 1966.

Another entrance at the northern end of the Keyham Steam Yard was opened on 19 July 1869. Some of the workmen were then compelled to use this gate — a great inconvenience because about 90% of the men lived to the south or west of the main southern gate. After many complaints, the Admiral Superintendent Rear Admiral Sir William King Hall, in November 1870, sought the wishes of the men — 575 said they wished to use the Albert Road gate and 244 the Ford gate. Notices were then posted at the muster boxes that the men were at liberty to use either gate.

Close to the gate, within a glass case, a gas light was fixed. An aperture was provided through which any workman could light his pipe, before or after leaving work, thereby avoiding carrying into the Yard matches which if found on him, led to instant dismissal.

Immediately inside the gate was the Yard's Call Bell — a bell cast in the Yard in 1859 — used to announce the start and finish of work. It was originally fixed to the top of a spar, but when the rope occasionally broke, a constable had to mount the pole to ring the bell. The exposed bell was later considered "unsightly", so in 1877 it was decided to place it behind the jalousie shutter in the tower above the gate opposite to the one that housed the clock.

In 1900 on Keyham Hill, the road outside the Yard was lowered six feet at one point and raised four feet at the bottom of the Hill. At the same time, the northern entrance to Keyham Yard was moved to its present position opposite St. Levan Road.

The beauty of the Albert Road Gate's construction raised demands for improving the entrance to South Yard. That entrance, at the bottom of Fore Street, had spacious gates for the workmen and a wicker gate alongside for officers and "strangers" — functional but not so ornate as that at Albert Road.

On entering South Yard, to the left, was this Yard's Call Bell. It was supported on a column 60 feet high made from the mainmast of an East Indiaman. The bell came from the "Tonnant", an 80 guns ship captured by Nelson in 1798 at the Battle of the Nile. Previously it had been stolen by the French from the Church of St. John in Malta.

In 1851, workmen of the Yard raised a petition to Lord John Hay, who as a Commodore, R.N.

MAIN GATE, H.M. DOCKYARD (NORTH), DEVONPORT.

Albert Road Gate to Keyham Yard

Dockyard Gates, Fore Street

Dockyard Gates, Fore St. Devonport.

was Superintendent. They wished to be relieved from "the mortifying and stupid ordeal" of taking off their hats on leaving the Yard to the policemen at the gate — to see that nothing was being carried out in, or under, their hats. The men were indignant, as it was not done at other Yards.

Dockyard men were allowed three minutes to get to their place of work after the bell stopped ringing. When, in 1893, the Admiralty tried to reduce that time to one minute, there was uproar. Representations were made and the old time allowance was restored.

That same year, the Devonport Mercantile Association petitioned the Admiralty to improve the entrance to the Dockyard at Fore Street "because it did not compare with Keyham Yard entrance". It was 1911 though before work actually began on demolishing the old buildings on either side of the gate. Then, on one side, a waiting room for visitors and new cells were built, and on the other, new commodious police quarters. The pillars of the gates were re-built simply by using the same stone re-faced. At the same time the bell was re-sited. It had been broken in 1891 and re-cast in the following year by John Warner and Sons of London. After being re-hung the bell was rung for the first time at the morning in-muster on 1 April, 1911.

In 1932 a new housing for the muster bell was erected at the Fore Street entrance. It had the appearance of granite, but was cleverly reconstructed in stone made locally by Mr. Charles Glenwalker, owner of the South Devon Concrete Manufacturing Company. In the base was carved

"This bell believed to be taken from a Spanish ship, was rung for muster for many years previous to 1924 when use of syrens began. It was broken in 1891 and re-cast. The 60 foot bell post was removed in 1931."

ALTERATIONS IN SOUTH YARD

At the end of 1853 it was announced that No. 2 slip at the Mutton Cove end of the Yard was to be lengthened to make it suitable for the ships which were being converted to take a screw. The fourth rate "Phoebe" being built on it had to be launched prior to lengthening because the slip was not long enough for the work to be carried out thereon.

The "Narcissus", 180 feet long, had been laid down on No. 1 slip during November, 1849. Having had her frames erected and been planked, she was lying to season — resting in the typical manner on a fir keel which would be replaced by an English elm one prior to launching — when, in March, 1857, it was decided to convert her to receive a screw propeller. Again this could not be done on the slip. It was first contemplated that she be launched and taken into dock to be lengthened, but after all, she was taken to pieces and the material used to build a longer ship on No. 3 slip from where she was launched as a screw steam frigate in October, 1959.

NEW LONG DOCK

In 1859 work commenced on the construction of a new Long Dock, formed from what had been the Double Dock. This was some thirty feet longer than the combined Head and Stern Docks. It was also 21 feet wider at the entrance and 14 feet greater in depth. The construction — carried out by Messrs. Kitt over a period of three years — lay below the water level at all states of the tide, so to enable the work to be carried out it was necessary to construct a circular cofferdam abutting against the old masonry wall on either side of the entrance.

By providing a groove outside the gates, a caisson from another part of the Yard could be put in place whenever it was necessary to lengthen the dock or for carrying out repairs to the inner set of two leafed gates. It is interesting to note the difference in the stone employed in these two positions. Whilst granite masonry was made to follow all round the caisson-bearing faces, it had been possible to economise in the way of the two leafed gates by providing Portland stone on the sill. This was probably the old Portland stone from the Double Dock, dressed and re-used in this position of lesser bearing pressure. Portland stone was also extensively used for facing the floor and walls of the dock, these blocks being laid on brickwork bedded directly on to the shillet rock.

RE-NUMBERING OF THE DOCKS

Soon after the completion of the Long Dock, the docks in South Yard, other than the original No. 1, were re-numbered.

The newly constructed Long Dock (ex-North Dock, combined with a slipway; ex-Double Dock, ex-Nos. 2 and 3) became No. 2.

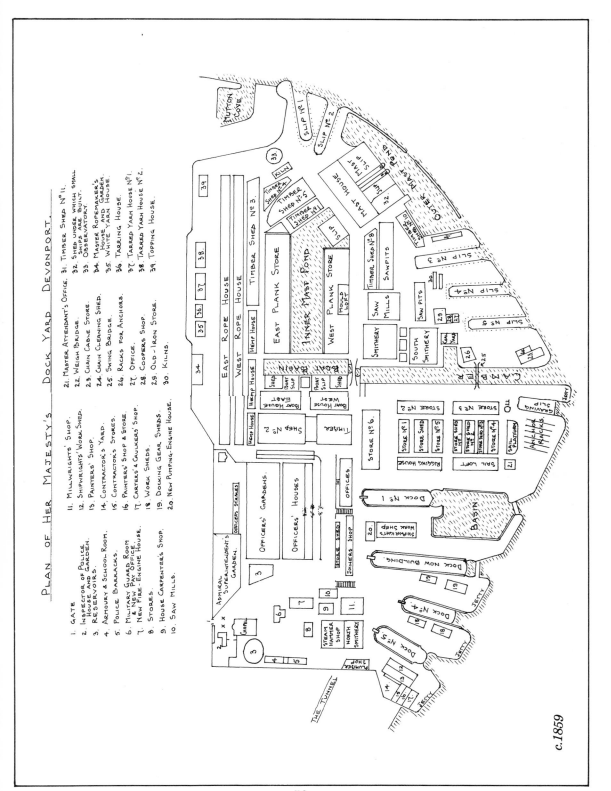

PLAN OF HER MAJESTY'S DOCK YARD DEVONPORT.

1. GATE.
2. INSPECTOR OF POLICE HOUSE AND GARDEN.
3. RESERVOIRS.
4. ARMOURY & SCHOOL ROOM.
5. POLICE BARRACKS.
6. MILITARY GUARD ROOM & NEW PAY OFFICE.
7. NEW FIRE-ENGINE HOUSE.
8. STORES.
9. HOUSE CARPENTER'S SHOP.
10. SAW MILLS.
11. MILLWRIGHTS' SHOP.
12. SHIPWRIGHTS' WORK SHED.
13. PAINTERS' SHOP.
14. CONTRACTOR'S YARD.
15. CONTRACTOR'S STORES.
16. PAINTERS' SHOP & STORE.
17. CARTERS' & CAULKERS' SHOP.
18. WORK SHEDS.
19. DOCKING GEAR SHEDS.
20. NEW PUMPING-ENGINE HOUSE.
21. MASTER ATTENDANT'S OFFICE.
22. WEIGH BRIDGE.
23. CHAIN CABLE STORE.
24. CHAIN CLEANING SHED.
25. SWING BRIDGE.
26. RACKS FOR ANCHORS.
27. OFFICE.
28. COOPERS' SHOP.
29. OLD-IRON STORE.
30. KILNS.
31. TIMBER SHED Nº 11.
32. SHED UNDER WHICH SMALL SHIPS ARE BUILT.
33. OBSERVATORY.
34. MASTER ROPEMAKER'S HOUSE AND GARDEN.
35. WHITE YARN HOUSE.
36. TARRING HOUSE.
37. TARRED YARN HOUSE Nº 1.
38. TARRED YARN HOUSE Nº 2.
39. TOPPING HOUSE.

c.1859

The North Dock (ex-Union, ex-No. 4) became No. 3.

The North New Dock (ex-New Union Dock, ex-No. 5) became No. 4.

Soon afterwards the docks in Keyham Steam Yard were numbered 5, 6 and 7.

FIRE IN THE SAW MILLS/STORE ROOM

On Thursday night, 24 November, 1864, a fire broke out in a building in South Yard. About 30 feet of the upper floor was occupied by a large amount of cabin furniture removed from ships paid off; and the ground floor was occupied by the steam saw mills. Part of it was also used as a Dining Hall.

The fire was discovered by a policeman on his beat. A window of the store room was broken in to allow hoses to be played on the fire. Eventually eight fire engines were in attendance, but they were unable to prevent the fire from breaking through the roof. The fire raged fiercely and concern was felt for the piles of timber stored alongside the Saw Mills and for the Rope Walk, Hemp Store and Boat House which were in the immediate vicinity.

Shortly after midnight the fire was under control, although by that time nearly all the furniture and most of the roof — much of which was glass — had been destroyed.

The fire appeared to have originated amongst the furniture, but by what means remained a mystery. The engines working the Saw Mill machinery was at the furthermost end of the building, about 100 feet away from the possible fire point. Some members of the Dockyard Volunteer Artillery were drilling in the room the previous evening until nearly nine o'clock, by gaslight, and were the last persons in the room prior to the fire.

The part of the store used as the men's Dining Hall remained undamaged, except from the large quantities of water which flowed in to it.

FIRST RELIGIOUS SERVICE AT A SHIP LAUNCH.

When the wooden paddle-wheel tug "Perseverance" was launched at a private ceremony on 19 January, 1875, a religious service compiled by the Archbishop of Canterbury, was used for the first time. The Admiralty then ordered that it be observed at the launching of all future ships.

NO. 4 DOCK ENTRANCE REPAIRED

Between 1874-76 a new granite sill was fitted at the entrance to No. 4 dock, and the gates replaced and re-hung. A large party of divers and labourers were engaged in the work, which necessitated a dam being built outside the gates to keep out the water. Great difficulty was at first experienced in erecting this dam, it being carried away several times. It was eventually made secure at a cost of several hundred pounds in providing extra bracings and stays, and in puddling it with some thousands of tons of clay — all of which having to be dredged up again afterwards.

The work carried out by contractor Mr. J. Pethick, was completed in September, 1876, when the first ship in the dock was the "Mount Edgcumbe". She entered dock on Wednesday 20 September to be converted to an Industrial Training Ship for Homeless and Destitute Boys in Devon and Cornwall. She became a familiar sight in the upper reaches of the River Tamar, being first moored off Saltash Passage and afterwards off Brunel Green, Saltash until 1920.

NO. 3 DOCK RECONSTRUCTED

In 1876 the major reconstruction of No. 3 dock commenced. Although the new No. 2 dock's construction had been remarkable for the greater use of pumps both in its construction and in its use, No. 3 dock must be singled out for its radical change in design.

The early form of graving docks had been with straight sides and the introduction of steps and altars, which followed the shape of the vessel, had been in the nature of an innovation. Custom reverted to its old practices when No. 3 dock was reconstructed with vertical sides. A large number of altars were still used, but no attempt was made to arrange them to a saucer shaped profile. Instead, they were housed underneath the arches which supported the decking above. The major reason for this was the introduction of steel built ships which had caused an alteration in the outline of the vessels to be docked. With the introduction of vertical sided ships, the need to arrange the steps to form a saucer profile disappeared.

Before the work commenced, the roof over the dock had to be removed. The sound portions of it were used in building a Coal Store. Then the old wooden jetties at the entrance had to be cut through and a cofferdam extended to the masonry walls.

The dock was to be made 386ft. 6 ins. in length, 95ft. breadth, 42ft. 11ins. depth, and 94 ft. wide at the entrance, transforming it into the largest dock west of London. The bottom was made slightly elevated in the centre sloping towards the ends, thus obviating the inconvenience previously met by the men working in the dock with the flat bottom being always wet. The culvert used for conveying water from the dock to the pumping engine had to be altered because the bottom of the new dock would be below the bottom of the present culvert. A new pumping house to cater for all four docks was erected at the north east corner of No. 1 dock.

The cost of the job was first estimated at £135,000, which was to be spread over the Naval Expenditure for 1876-7-8-9. The work was to be carried out by contract — Mr. J. Pethick of Norley Buildings, Plymouth — but supervised by the Director of the Works Department. The contractor was allowed the use of the floor at the east end of the Boat Store as a mould loft for setting out the work. Most of the granite required for the work was obtained from Messrs. Freeman's quarry at Penryn.

Unfortunately, progress was hindered by the effects of a heavy gale in October, 1877, the cofferdam across the entrance being almost demolished. To improve protection, a ship was used as a breakwater. Then at the beginning of November, 1878, a serious landslip occurred. The construction of this dock between two others only left a space of about 200 feet. The ridge on the northern side next to No. 4 dock gave way, entirely destroying a tramway which ran along it and partially filling up the new dock.

The foundation stone was formally laid on 11 December, 1878 by the Admiral Superintendent, Rear Admiral G.O. Willes, but a few days later the new dock was the scene of an even more extensive landslip. A watchman, shortly after midnight on Sunday 15th, heard several sharp reports on the south side of the work. He discovered several baulks of timber, erected some time before to carry a tram-road — (an inclined road by which the excavated material was drawn in trucks to the surface) — and a steam traveller crane, had been forced bodily into the dock by an extensive slip of many thousands of tons of rock. The whole of the south side of the dock, which had been shaped down and was nearly ready to receive the masonry, was found to have bodily subsided. A mass of stone, 250ft. long, 12ft. wide and 30ft. deep, equal to 90,000 cu. ft., had shifted from its required position carrying with it several thousand pounds worth of plant.

Concurrent with the above, a fissure opened in the main road of the Yard at the head of the dock. Being nearly 30ft. from the line of excavation, the fissure — about 5ft. long and 3ft. wide — indicated that thousands of tons of rock from that end had also drifted towards the dock. The rock in its descent carried away water mains resulting in tons of water flowing into the dock, too.

A rough estimate of the damage placed the cost at £50,000 — but even more important, it added two years to the work period. The cause of this accident was attributed to the wet and frosty weather acting forcibly upon the slatey character of the rock.

The new caisson for No. 3 Dock was successfully floated into position on 12 July, 1882. Water between caisson and cofferdam was then pumped out to allow the remainder of the rock that obstructed the entrance to the dock to be blasted away.

The machinery for pumping out the dock was constructed by Messrs. Easton and Anderson of Whitehall Place, London, and Erith. Trials of the pumps — two centrifugal pumps worked by a fan, 7ft. 6 ins. diameter, driving direct on to the pump spindle by a pair of horizontal compound engines — were carried out on Thursday 20th March, 1884. The trials commenced at 6.50 a.m. and, as predicted, the dock was emptied of 39,000 tons of water within four hours.

When the dock was finished it was found that the jetties either side of the entrance were in a very poor state. No further contract for their renewal was invited, but the work — which lasted for many months — was done by "Government Day Work". Furthermore, when the Lords of the Admiralty made their annual visit to Devonport in October, 1884, they were informed that the dock could still not be used because it had not been fitted with capstans and other gear necessary for docking ships. The local officials were ordered to get on with fitting them as speedily as possible.

On 25 November, 1884 the new No. 3 Dock came into use when the gunvessel "Reindeer", which had been launched just twelve months earlier, entered it preparatory to being commissioned by Commander G.L. Atkinson for the East Indies station.

CHAPTER 10

THE METROPOLITAN POLICE ARRIVE

After many complaints against the "Dockyard Coppers" as they had become known, an enquiry was conducted into their activities by Superintendent T.M. Mallalieu of the Metropolitan Police. His comprehensive findings, amongst which was the opinion that the Dockyard Police Force was ill-trained, resulted in their disbandment. In 1860 an Act of Parliament laid down that the policing of all Royal Dockyards should be carried out by the Metropolitan Police.

Control of policing in Devonport Dockyard was transferred on Monday 22 October, 1860 to the Metropolitan Force under the superintendence of Mr. Bray. He was a former Chief of Police at the House of Lords and a former detective in attendance on Her Majesty Queen Victoria.

The number of constables who came from London was 34 and about 30 were retained from the former force. Those policemen belonging formerly to the Dockyard Police but disqualified from entering the Metropolitan Force, were allowed to enter the Yard as labourers.

In November, 1859 it had been planned to form a Water Police branch. Three sergeants and nine privates were to be selected from the force in Devonport and Keyham Yards, and they were to use the hulk "Endymion" as their rendezvous. However, that rôle was also taken over by the Metropolitan Police. They were originally accommodated in the "Algeria" berthed off New Passage. In May, 1864 she was replaced by the hulk of the larger ship "Leda", a former fifth rate vessel built at Pembroke in 1828. She was moored in the Hamoaze, off the Gun Wharf, and for over forty years provided accommodation for the men and their families. At first the police rowed the river, but later acquired the luxury of steam pinnaces.

In the 1890's resentment grew amongst the Metropolitan Policemen because it had been ordered that they could not continue to serve if any relative was employed at any Government establishment within fifteen miles of their own job. For example, if a Police Officer in the Yard became related by marriage to an employee at Bull Point, one or the other had to seek alternative employment. Two Inspectors of Police were moved, one just because his son became a fitter apprentice.

In 1897 the Admiralty directed that the Metropolitan Police in the Yard should have sole charge of firefighting. Hitherto steam and manual fire engines had been under the charge of Dockyard mechanics and labourers, a party of whom having to be on "Fire Duty" night and day. It was approved to add an Inspector and six Constables to the establishment, provide them with quarters and uniforms and that they be known as the "Fire Party".

CONTROL AND MANAGEMENT OF H.M. NAVAL YARDS

In 1860 Commissioners were appointed by the Admiralty to inquire into the Control and Management of Her Majesty's Naval Yards, and their report was presented to both Houses of Parliament in the following year. Many senior Dockyard officers were interviewed, including the Superintendent of Devonport Yard, Rear Admiral Sir Thomas S. Pasley, Bart.

The Commissioners reported that

(a) the system of control and management was inefficient;

(b) the purchase of stores was unsatisfactory; and

(c) the system of accounts was elaborate and minute, but so far as they could judge, its results were not to be relied upon.

On the cost of building and converting ships, they were unable to express a view.

Fire Party at the ready

"We are of the opinion that the system of "Task and Job", as at present carried on in the Dockyards is open to great abuse. It is based upon schemes of prices consisting of 94,762 items. This can hardly fail to lead to numerous errors in pricing the work done. Another grave objection is the multiplicity of measurements required."

Admiral Pasley's opinion of "Task and Job" was that one third extra work was done and the men earned one third more, the highest wages for a shipwright being 6/- a day, the average 5/9d. He was not in favour of the adoption of "Task and Job with unlimited earnings", because it brought out any reserve and left nothing to fall back on. He preferred "Task and Job" for emergencies only, the best system for ordinary times being "Day Pay with checked measurements".

The system of pay in the Keyham Steam Yard was different to the rest of the Yard. Men in the Pay Clerk's Office, who were termed Work Collectors, visited each man at his place of work every day, took details of the work on which he was employed and the time spent upon it. The Leading Man of each shop looked down that list with the Work Collector to be sure that the man had booked his time to proper service. This formed the basis of the cost of labour and from it the wages were made up weekly. John Trickett, the Chief Engineer and Inspector of Steam Machinery at Devonport, reported to the Commissioners that the system worked well.

The Commissioners reported:—

"The policy of converting a large number of sailing ships to screws can only be justified by the necessity which existed of constructing a screw navy with the least delay."

James P. Peake, Master Shipwright at Devonport, had stated in his evidence that conversion to steam may not be economical but it saved time. He felt that if time had been available, the vast sums of money expended in conversion would have been better applied to building new ships. One difficulty was the shortage of the right size oak timber.

PROGRESS IN SHIP CONSTRUCTION

For many reasons, 1860 can well be taken as the year from which to observe the notable progress made in warship construction and marine engineering, concurrently with the corresponding progress in the Dockyard.

With the introduction of armour, an Armour Plate shop was established in the Quadrangle at Keyham, with the necessary furnace for heating plates $4\frac{1}{2}$ ins. in thickness which were to be fitted to the "Ocean". The armour was fitted to the sides of the ship in No. 6 Dock at Keyham, with the aid of the travelling crane which operated on rails specially fitted for the purpose on each side of the dock.

The "Ocean" was the first armour-plated vessel built in the Yard. She had actually been laid down as a wooden line-of-battle ship but after much progress had been made on her, the Admiralty directed that she — along with her sister ships "Prince Consort", "Caledonia" and "Royal Alfred" — be converted to iron clads. In the construction of these ships, iron beams and deck plating were used for the first time. During conversion which commenced on 3 June, 1861, the "Ocean" was lengthened by being cut in two amidships, the fore part being then hauled up the slip about twenty feet and five additional pairs of frames inserted. The original framework of her stem and stern was also taken down and made sharper. The hull received a complete casing of iron armour tapering in thickness from $4\frac{1}{2}$ ins. at the level of the upper deck to 3 ins. at six feet below the waterline.

The iron masts for the "Ocean" were brought to Devonport by rail and sea. After being forged by Messrs. Finch and Heath of Chepstow for the contractor Mr. Ferguson of London, the main mast 116 feet long; the foremast 83 feet long and the shorter mizzen mast were loaded on to railway trucks for the journey from Chepstow, via Swindon, Bristol, Exeter and Millbay in Plymouth. They were shipped from the G.W.R. Docks at Millbay in Government "lumps" to Keyham Yard.

The Admiralty had hoped to use more of the larger wooden ships by cutting them down and armour-plating them. An Order was given in August, 1870 to Devonport Yard to so convert the "Robust", but in August, 1872 the Admiralty changed their minds and ordered that the "Robust" be taken to pieces.

The first examples from Devonport of composite shipbuilding — iron frames for a timber hull — were the "Flirt" and "Fly", which were both launched on the same day, 20

December, 1867. They were also among the first class of ships to have twin screws. These ships had been designed for service in China, to combine a shallow draught, 7ft. 6ins., with a heavy armament, 7in. guns. One propeller would have had too big a diameter for the shallow draught.

For some years, Devonport ceased to be a first class shipbuilding Yard. Its workload dropped to make it little more than a repair establishment. It meant the discharge of many artisans, but to ease their problems the Admiralty announced that they would grant free passages for them to travel to Quebec in the steam transports "Serapis" and "Crocodile", which were sailing to bring home troops. The men were warned though that they would be in the same position as ordinary emigrants and the Government would in no way be responsible for providing employment. However, there was a great demand for labour by private employers in the Quebec area, so several men from Devonport and other Yards applied. Although passage was being offered free, the men were still expected to pay the cost of victualling and other incidental expenses whilst on passage — estimated at £2. 5s. 0d. per adult and half for children. Some of the men were prepared to pay but as the majority had no means of doing so, the Mayor of Devonport, John Rolston, made a public appeal for funds on their behalf.

At the Dockyards

Present titles	Proposed titles
Master Shipwright and Engineer, or Master Shipwright.	Chief Constructor.
Assistant Master Shipwrights.	Constructors.

At the Admiralty

Present titles	Proposed titles
Chief Naval Architect.	Director of Naval Construction.
Surveyor of Dockyards.	Surveyor of Dockyard and Chief Constructor.
Constructors.	Chief Constructors.
Professional Assistant to Surveyor of Dockyards (held by an Assistant Master Shipwright).	Constructor and Professional Assistant to Surveyor of Dockyards.
Chief Draughtsman.	Assistant Constructor and Chief Draughtsman.
Second Class Draughtsman (acting as Professional Secretary to the Council of Construction.)	Assistant Constructor.

OFFICERS' TITLES CHANGED

By an Order in Council dated 13 May, 1875, the Admiralty announced that they had had under consideration the salaries, titles and positions of the Principal Officers of the Shipwright and Engineer Departments in the Dockyards. They admitted that the duties and responsibilities of the Master Shipwrights and their Assistants had increased in recent years, and were far more varied than they used to be "consequent of the change from wood to iron shipbuilding and of the numerous changes in the construction and armament of H.M. Ships of War."

They therefore proposed that their salaries be increased and at the same time to introduce the following uniformity of designation throughout the officers of the Constructive Departments in the Dockyards and at the Admiralty:—

TIMBER TO STEEL

Consequent on the many changes in shipbuilding, the large stacks of oak timber formerly kept in open sheds where they remained to season until required, were reduced. The old saw pits fell into disuse, as the new saw mills, built 1857-58, were able to meet the reduced requirement. The steam kiln, the timber storehouses and covered sheds where other timber had been stored, were removed and replaced with open racks for storing steel plates.

The Smithery in South Yard was extended and to drive the extra machinery fitted there, use was made of the engines of the gunvessel "Pigeon" which was being broken up. They were adapted in the Fitting Shop at Keyham for their new role.

The building of "Curlew" and "Landrail" in 1885-86 saw a further development when mild steel replaced iron as a material for shipbuilding.

When first tried in 1881 for parts of the hull of the corvette "Heroine", it raised much doubt, for it frequently occurred that mild steel plates, after being heated and worked into shape and placed into position one day, would on the next morning be found to be seriously fractured, especially after a cold frosty night. The Admiralty, in conjunction with the steel makers conducted very extensive experiments and research. The failure was found to be chiefly due to over-heating of the metal and to prevent such failure it was ordered that the metal should not be heated beyond a certain limiting temperature, and that it was essential it be gradually cooled afterwards.

To prevent corrosion of the internal plating which was likely to come into contact with bilge water — such as floor plates, lower plating of bulkheads, etc. — saw the introduction of the procedure of "galvanising". This was first introduced at Devonport during the construction of the third class cruiser "Serpent", which was laid down in November, 1885 and launched in 1887. She left Plymouth on 8 November, 1890, but forty eight hours later, through an error of navigation, she was wrecked on the north coast of Spain, and only three ratings survived.

Under the Naval Defence Act of 1889, provision was made for the construction of eighteen torpedo gunboats. One of the first — "Antelope" — was laid down at Devonport on 21 October, 1889, but she was on the slipway a considerable time due to the shortage of shipwrights and because contractors could not be found willing to build the machinery. This was eventually undertaken by Messrs. Yarrow of Poplar in 1892 and "Antelope" was launched on 12 July, 1893.

The shortage of shipwrights had arisen because that year, 1889, had seen the laying down of the third class protected cruisers "Phoebe" (in April) and "Philomel" (in May). The situation was further complicated with the laying down in June of the first class protected cruiser "Edgar". Of 7,350 tons and 360 feet long, she became the then largest ship to be built at Devonport. With her construction, the limiting capacity of the existing building slips had been reached, for the clearance in launching this ship from No. 5 slip was but a few inches on each side.

Usually, when vessels were launched, all the men in the Yard could witness it. However, on many occasions, when permission was granted to leave their work to attend a launch, the men would leave the Yard. So, to witness the launch of the "Edgar", 24 November, 1890, only workmen employed on the slip or in the vicinity were allowed to attend. They were ordered to work overtime during three dinner hours to make up for this "great privilege" — of witnessing the launching of the vessel they had built.

FIRE ON BOARD H.M.S. THETIS

The large wooden ram-bow corvette "Thetis" was launched at Devonport on 26 October, 1871. After being named by Miss A. Codrington, daughter of Admiral Sir Henry Codrington, Commander-in-Chief, Devonport, the ship floated beautifully but too far into the stream. Her anchor was not let go in time to prevent her stern striking the quarter of the "Royal Adelaide", Admiral Codrington's own flagship moored in the Hamoaze. Luckily little damage was done to either ship.

Just before 9 p.m. on Monday 10 March, 1879, a Metropolitan Policeman saw smoke emanating from the "Thetis" which was then lying in the south west corner of No. 3 Basin at Keyham. He immediately gave the alarm to a number of men on board her, who were working overtime in order to finish the vessel for commissioning at the end of that week.

Fire had broken out in a store-room which was full of paint, cordage, sails, etc. — stores which had only been embarked over the previous week-end. A party of about 40 sailors and marines were sent from the Receiving Hulk "Vengeance" which was moored nearby. Rockets were sent up and guns fired as signals for other ships in harbour to send further assistance.

The "Thetis" was warped around to bring her head to the north so that with the wind blowing from the south, the flames were prevented from sweeping over her.

Immense quantities of water, estimated at over 2,000 tons, were poured into her. However, when this amount of water caused the ship to settle, some of the pumps which had been pumping water in had their roles switched to pump water out. It was between 4 and 5 a.m. Tuesday morning before the fire was extinguished, and a further four hours later before all the water was pumped out of her.

The fire was believed to have been caused by the ignition of some waste material that had been left lying around — a neglect of supervisory duties that caused the Admiralty to censor some officers.

The departure of "Thetis" was delayed for six weeks. It had been intended she sail urgently for the East Coast of Africa Station to relieve the "Tenedos" which was expected to return home for repairs after running on to a shoal at the mouth of Tugela River. After the fire damage had been repaired "Thetis" commissioned on 13 May, 1879 and sailed on 5 June for the Pacific where she spent the next four years.

ANOTHER GREAT FIRE IN SOUTH YARD

Just before 4 p.m. on Wednesday, 8 February, 1882 the whole of Devonport and neighbourhood were aroused by news that a great fire was raging in the Dockyard. The centre building in the large "quadrangle" of store houses was in flames. This store, the Return Junk and Hemp Store, two storeys high and built of wood, was filled with many tons of oakum, old rope, tens of thousands of wedges and other articles of equally inflammable nature. It was bounded on three sides by large high stone-built storehouses and on the fourth side by the Rigging House and Sail Loft.

The first indication of the fire was given by two caulkers named Chappell and Shepheard, who were working in the Oakum Store. Very shortly the Dockyard steam fire engine arrived, followed by one from Keyham, and several hand engines. By this time an enormous mass of flame and dense smoke was rising into the sky which obviated any need to fire guns to give warning to the Garrison troops and ships in the harbour. At one time great fear prevailed that surrounding buildings might be affected.

An official report of the fire was telegraphed to the Admiralty and an investigation into its cause was also held. One theory was that it originated through "spontaneous combustion" amongst the oakum, some of which had been lying in the store for a long time. Some time earlier, on the instructions of the Admiralty, the oakum had been removed from a fire-proof building and placed in this store which the local Dockyard

officers had said was not a suitable site.

Another theory was that the fire was "pre-arranged". At the exact spot where the fire began, was stowed the last consignment of picked oakum which the Admiralty always received from prisons. This last consignment came from Dublin Prison and it was suggested that the centre of one of the bales had been deliberately made damp or that some inflammable substance had been inserted in it prior to shipment.

An official inquiry into the cause of the fire was held at the offices of the Admiral Superintendent. Captain A.J. Chatfield, of the Steam Reserve, presided, in the absence, on leave, of the Admiral Superintendent, Rear Admiral C.T. Curme. No decision was made, but it was concluded the fire may have been caused by spontaneous combustion of the oakum.

MORE ALTERATIONS IN SOUTH YARD

In 1889 the gates of No. 1 dock had to be lifted for repair. To enable this to be done, the contractors, Messrs. Lapthorn and Goad, built a dam in the basin outside the dock, which enabled the gates to be removed and docked in their own dock. The job was completed in October, 1890.

Before the second class protected cruiser "Aeolus" was laid down on No. 2 slip on 10 March, 1890, the slip was lengthened. Even so, when she was launched in November, 1891, her bows extended beyond the shed covering the slip.

In October of the same year work commenced on lengthening No. 3 dock, it being extended by 36 feet to within a few feet of the railway line at the head of the dock. A 30 ton travelling crane was also fitted on each side of the dock. Work which lasted several months, actually commenced with the battleship "Anson" in the dock but it was found necessary to undock her when blasting operations commenced. A temporary tramway was laid down to the riverside jetty to assist disposal of the rubble in to barges.

IMPROVED LIGHTING

In March, 1890 provision was made to light the ships, then under construction, by gas. It was felt that this would be of great benefit whenever overtime was required, particularly during the winter months. The work was carried out by Mr.

R.E. Couch of Fore Street, Devonport, at a cost of £500.

In November, 1892 new gas mains were laid on each side of No. 2 slip to provide extra flares for night work. These new mains also enabled officers to check the consumption of gas, which was supplied by the local Corporation at a big discount off the usual price.

In the next couple of years, experiments were carried out by Mr. Welch, Assistant Constructor, to light the ships in South Yard by electricity. It had already been done at Portsmouth and Chatham, although the trial at the latter Yard was abandoned for being too costly. Portsmouth though, at this time, had several ships lit by electricity. When the "Edgar" was fitting out in Keyham Yard, a portable dynamo was placed on board with a boiler alongside. It could light about 350 lamps distributed throughout the ship. It was estimated that to light the "Edgar" cost £2 a day, including the wages of the men supervising the plant. This was considered expensive, in spite of the fact that the candles formerly used cost nearly as much.

At the end of 1897 though, the Admiralty called for plans and estimates for the complete electrical lighting of Devonport and Keyham Yards. The system was designed and erected under the supervision of Messrs. Preece and Cardew, of Westminster, consulting electrical engineers to the Admiralty. The foundations of the power generating station at Keyham were commenced on 24 March, 1904 by Messrs. Lapthorn and Company. The building 240ft. 9ins. long by 80ft. wide, together with a 200ft. high chimney, required two million bricks — including 25,000 special fire bricks — and cost £50,000. It was divided into two parts — a boiler house and an engine room. Within the former were fitted seven sets of Babcock and Wilcox's water tube boilers, all self stoking; and in the engine room, three engines of 1,000 H.P. and one of 500 H.P. Another 1,000 H.P. engine was added later.

During the implementation of the scheme, in March, 1903, the Admiralty transferred the supervision of electrical work from the Constructive staff to a separate department under an Electrical Engineer. The use of electricity increased so rapidly that within five years the staff of the Electrical Engineer's Department had reached 1,300.

The electrical installation work was virtually completed by 1906, although it was nearly two years later — July, 1908 — before the Admiralty gave approval to light the tunnel between the Yards.

UNIFORM WORKING WEEK?

One effect of the installation of electric light was the decision of the Admiralty to introduce a uniform working week throughout the year. Hitherto the hours had varied according to the season; the length of the working day being regulated by the period of daylight — longer in the summer, shorter in the winter. By the provision of electricity for all parts of the Yard, the importance of daylight for carrying on the work of the establishment was so greatly minimised that the need to alter the working hours no longer existed.

Before deciding how the 48 working hours would be arranged the Admiralty decided to seek the views of the men and allow them to vote in favour of one of two schemes. Both schemes provided for work to commence at 7 a.m. and the schemes only differed in regard to the afternoon muster on Fridays. Under Scheme A the dinner time on Fridays was to be the same as on other days — noon to 1.30 p.m.; while under Scheme B it was to be reduced to 45 minutes — noon to 12.45 p.m. The payment of wages under the latter scheme would take place at the p.m. out-muster instead of at noon.

Scheme B received an overwhelming majority; 5,379 voting for it, compared with 1,129 for Scheme A. The number of non-voters totalled 1,100. Portsmouth and Chatham voted similarly so recommendations were made to the Admiralty to adopt Scheme B.

In June though, in spite of the result of the poll, the Admiralty decided to please themselves and inaugurate their own scheme with 45 minutes dinner time every day. They issued "Summer" and "Winter" tables, the former period running 1 February to 31 October.

There would not be any out-muster at Friday noon, and the men's wages would be paid at the afternoon out-muster. Naturally there was some grumbling over the new scheme, although the majority were not greatly bothered.

MUTTON COVE GATE

On Monday, 14 January, 1884 a sub-committee of the General Purposes Committee of the

Devonport Town Council, including the Mayor, called on Mr. James Angear, Chief Constructor in the Yard, with a proposal for a new entrance into the Yard for men living at the southern end of the town. It would mean a great saving in the time involved for the double journey between Fore Street gate and the building slips at the Mutton Cove end of the Yard.

It was some years later though before a position for a gate was chosen in the wall opposite the end of Pembroke Street. This proved impracticable because of the siting of the buildings on the inside of the wall at that point. A new site was then chosen opposite the Roman Catholic Church in James Street.

The new gates opened for the first time on 8 June, 1891 — but only for the morning entry because the Dockyard Police said they could not cope with manning another gate. In September, a Search Office was built at the gate although it was still not available for exit.

In 1898 representations were made to the Admiralty, and a deputation from Devonport Town Council even journeyed to the House of Commons, to request that Mutton Cove gate be opened for entry and exit. Mr. Austen Chamberlain, the Civil Lord of the Admiralty, would not agree because "little advantage would accrue to the workmen and none to the public service."

Seven years later, Vice Admiral W.H. Henderson directed that "an experiment be tried in allowing the gate to be used for entering and leaving the Yard at dinner time. If sufficient men use it, it will become a permanent arrangement" — which it did.

ANOTHER BIG FIRE

On Saturday, 16 June, 1894 South Yard was the scene of an alarming conflagration which resulted in the total destruction of a large storehouse principally used for the storage of iron and steel. The fire was first noticed and the alarm raised at about 10.30 p.m. by P.C. Vogwell of the Dockyard Police. From the outset there was very little chance of saving the building, one of the few wooden storehouses left in the Yard. About 150 feet long and 50 feet wide, its contents included several valuable coils of steel hawsers, from one to four inches in diameter, some thousands of nuts and bolts, and sheets and bars of iron. Many of

these items bore evidence of the intensity of the heat generated by the fire, immense pieces of iron being bent and steel rope twisted into unimaginable shapes.

Fire appliances from military and naval establishments arrived in quick succession, and the Devonport and Stonehouse Fire Brigades also attended although they were not actually used. By the combined efforts of the Dockyard Police and hundreds of sailors, the fire was under control soon after midnight.

How the fire originated was a complete mystery. The building had been locked up and everything left apparently safe when work had ceased at 2 o'clock on that Saturday afternoon. The building had been passed several times after this, but it was some 8 or 9 hours later that P.C. Vogwell observed the first indications of a fire — a fire that was to cause thousands of pounds worth of damage.

CHAPTER 11

DEVONPORT'S FIRST BATTLESHIP

The laying down of the battleship "Ocean" in the Diamond Jubilee Year of Queen Victoria, marked the beginning of a new era for the western yard. To enable the "Ocean" to be built one of the slipways had to be lengthened. In June, 1896 the Admiralty invited tenders to extend No. 3 slip which had just had its roof taken off. The wood covering provided protection from the rain so some of the men did not relish the prospect of being subjected to all winds and weathers. On the other hand shipbuilding on open slipways commended itself to other men because the conditions were far more healthy than being under cover. Work on the extension commenced in August, 1896.

Much preliminary work on the "Ocean" was done before the ship's keel was laid on 15 February, 1897. Instructions were given that she be completed within 20 months. An incentive in hastening her construction was what became known as "The Canopus Stakes" a shipbuilding "race" between the Royal Dockyards building "Canopus" class battleships — "Canopus" at Portsmouth; "Goliath" at Chatham; and "Ocean" at Devonport. Devonport started five weeks after the other two Yards and suffered a serious set-back when some of the ship's frames collapsed. It appears that the framework had been left insecure when two gangs of men were removed to assist in docking the battleship "Colossus". The ribs of the ship fell like a pack of cards; about 90 feet of the fore part of the ship — from the stem to the turret — collapsed, over 100 tons of material being dislodged. At the official inquiry, a labourer confessed that he removed a bolt which had been keeping some frames in position until the plating and riveting had been completed. The man was ignorant of the consequences of his action, his object in removing the bolt being to facilitate the passage of some iron plates he was conveying to another part of the ship. An examination of the loosened bolt showed it to be intact — that it had been unscrewed — and not wrenched off.

Other vexatious delays occurred — shortage of drillers and riveters; a strike in the engineering trades; non-delivery of the principal castings such as the stem, stern post, rudder, shaft brackets, etc. Consequently, the "Ocean" was on the slip for 17 months, twice as long as expected. Although her launching weight was not the heaviest on record, she was heavier per foot length than any vessel hitherto launched in a Government Yard. To reduce the risk at her launch, the slip was further lengthened 20 - 30 feet into the Hamoaze, by dredging the entrance to the slip and extending the concrete bed. She was finally launched on 5 July, 1898 by H.R.H. Princess Louise.

Five other battleships were built on this slip — "Implacable", "Bulwark", "Montagu", "Queen", and "King Edward VII". Work in "Implacable" actually commenced on No. 2 slip, her frames being bolted together so that they could easily be taken down and moved to No. 3 slip after "Ocean" had been launched. "Implacable" was launched on 11 March, 1899 in the presence of the Crown Prince of Siam, and was first commissioned in September 1901 for service in the Mediterranean.

Battleships were launched almost annually from Devonport Yard from 1898 until 1914. One remarkable achievement being the fact that "Bulwark" was actually launched within seven months of being laid down.

OTHER WORK AS A RESULT OF "OCEAN"

Other work consequent on the building of "Ocean" was (a) the extension to No. 1 jetty; (b) the extension to No. 2 dock; (c) the extension of the railway system; and (d) erection of a new Machine Shop, Drawing Office and Mould Loft. The Drawing Office was erected in 1898 alongside the main road with a new Mould Loft adjoining, replacing the previous office built in 1779.

No. 1 Jetty had been formed when the disused Graving Slip, situated just north of the Camber entrance, was filled in during 1894. Vessels placed on this slip had their keels subjected to severe battering until the tide had receded sufficiently to allow them to settle upon the blocks. In 1877, the owners of the river steamer "Aeriel" refused to allow their vessel to be submitted to such treatment when the Dockyard were going to repair her after a collision with a steam launch attached to Keyham Factory. She had to be docked instead.

No. 1 Jetty had, so far, been little used because of its limited access. During the course of its extension, blasting operations were carried out off the Jetty to allow deeper draught vessels to lie alongside. Another important feature, carried out by Messrs. Hill and Co., of Plymouth, was the fitting of an enormous set of sheer legs which could lift up to 100 tons. For some time the Admiralty were unable to decide whether to have the new sheers erected on a projecting or flush jetty. However, in view of the great strain which lifting such heavy weights would bring to bear, the decision was made in favour of a flush jetty. The sheers, ordered from Messrs. Cowans, Sheldon and Co. of Carlisle, had two front legs each 156 feet in length and 54 inches in diameter, and a back leg 202 feet in length and 63 inches in diameter. Worked by steam supplied from an engine house built on the jetty, they were erected on 4 March, 1898, and remained until January, 1937. Then, before a large crowd of spectators including the Commander-in-Chief, Devonport, Admiral the Hon. Sir Reginald A.R. Plunkett-Ernle-Erle-Drax, the after retaining leg of the sheers was cut loose and the whole lot allowed to fall into the Hamoaze. There, tugs pulled them clear of the fairway.

NEW SHEER LEGS AT KEYHAM

In 1898 a new set of sheer legs was ordered to replace those on the east side of No. 3 Basin at Keyham which had collapsed. When the screw ship "Temeraire" was being moved in the basin, her bowsprit struck one of the legs causing another leg to collapse and the sheers to fall into the Basin. After this accident, a survey was made of the other set on the west side of the Basin. These were also condemned so two replacement sets were ordered. Those for the east side were actually purchased second hand. The manufacturers would therefore not accept responsibility for their erection, so the work was done under the supervision of Mr. J. Gale, Leading Man of Labourers in the Yard.. He used the old sheers to raise the new, and the new ones to remove the old. The set fitted on the west side of the Basin overhanging the Hamoaze, were demolished in 1915.

It was thought that the new sheers at Keyham would help with the fitting-out of "Bulwark" and "Implacable", but it was found that it was not safe to squeeze those ships through the entrance to the basin to berth them on the inside wall where the sheer legs were erected. When the Basin was built it was not anticipated that ships would have such great beams. It was suggested that the entrance be widened but this would have put the Basin and three docks out of action for months. Nothing was done because it was felt that the situation would be eased when the Keyham Extension, further north, was completed.

However, the value of the sheer legs at Keyham was proved when they were used to lift an American torpedo boat out of the water. The "Somers" which, under neutrality rules, had been laid up in Mylor Creek, Falmouth, during the Spanish-American War, was lifted on to the deck of the steamer "Manhattan" for shipment back to the United States.

NO. 2 DOCK ENLARGED

In January, 1897 work commenced on extensive alterations to No. 2 Dock (formerly the Double Dock). It was carried out by contractors, Messrs. G. Shellabear and Son. These alterations were rendered necessary owing to the dock, as constructed in 1859, being now too narrow at the bottom to accommodate the modern ships, particularly cruisers fitted with bilge keels. It was therefore decided to cut out all the lower Portland stone altars to a height of 15 feet from floor level, and after excavating the rock at the back to a more perpendicular line, to fill in this portion of the sides with new granite altars set to a steeper pitch thus giving the dock an additional width of about 17 feet at floor level. Over 100,000 cubic feet of granite was used, all of it being supplied from Penryn Quarries; upwards of 2,000,000 bricks were used to form the backings on which the granite was fixed; and an additional 1,000,000 used in enlarging the culverts at the sides of the dock.

When the work on widening was nearly complete, it was decided to lengthen the dock by about 40 feet at the head to accommodate the rams of battleships. The completed dock alterations were accepted by the Admiralty in May, 1898. The dock, now $460\frac{1}{2}$ feet long and 73 feet wide at the entrance, was capable of holding any class of ship then in the Navy except the two cruisers "Powerful" and "Terrible". The first ship in the dock was "Niobe" who was placed therein to have her bottom sheathed with copper and her submerged torpedo tubes fitted.

NO. 3 DOCK EXTENDED

In May, 1898, tenders were invited for similarly extending No. 3 Dock, in spite of the fact that £10,000 had been spent as recently as October, 1890 in lengthening it by 36 feet. Now it was found that it lacked width at the fore end where it had been extended.

A NEW BUILDING SLIP

That same year, 1898, it was planned to make extensive alterations to No. 5 slip — the northernmost one from which the cruiser "Psyche" had been launched on 19 July — in order to provide facilities for the building of a second battleship. The only slip then available for such a purpose was No. 3 on which the keel of the "Implacable" had been laid six days earlier. However, a survey of No. 5 slip satisfied the authorities that the extension was impracticable as the work would have involved the demolition of the Smithery and other permanent buildings.

An alternative scheme — the building of an entirely new slip — was undertaken at a point which had the advantage that vessels built on it would be launched into the widest part of the Hamoaze. Situated between the two old building sheds at the southern end of the Yard (Nos. 1 and 2 slips) and No. 3 slip on which "Ocean" and "Montagu" had been built, were the old mast ponds and timber sheds. These facilities had been well suited for the building of wooden ships — but had then become obsolete. The mast ponds were accordingly filled in and a considerably sized area of land cleared, including the timber sheds, plank houses, etc. Five of the old mast houses were demolished but two new ones were built in their stead.

The slip was designed by, and executed under the supervision of, Major E.R. Kenyon, R.E. Superintendent Engineer of the Yard, with Mr. C. Millard as Civil Engineer and Mr. J. Bazley, Clerk of Works.

Work on clearing the site commenced in July, 1900. The original plan was for a slip 450 feet in length but after the work had started the dimensions were increased to 600 feet long by 90 feet wide. Furthermore, allowance was also made in the foundations for any future extensions up to 155 feet.

The stone floor was carried well out into the river to prevent any possibility of the largest ships touching the sea bottom before floating. For constructing this underwater part of the slip a temporary cofferdam was built about twenty yards out in the river.

The foundations were of a complicated nature in that the slip was being built partly on the site of the canal which once connected the old mast ponds; partly on the site of a mast house which had a pair of slips sloping in opposite directions; and partly on the reclaimed areas of the inner and outer mast ponds. The gradient of the slip was 1 in 19 and with the head of the slip about 30 feet above rock level and sited on a portion of the inner mast pond, it was necessary to construct re-inforced concrete arches founded on rock to carry that end of the slip.

The difficulties encountered by the engineers in laying the floor of the slip were also greater than anticipated. The site had been selected in the belief that a fine bed of limestone was there, but during the course of blasting — in the construction of passages from one side of the slip to the other — it was found that the rock was very much fissured and water springs were discovered in several places. With great ingenuity though, the difficulties were overcome by diverting the course of some springs and laying pipes to carry off the water from others. Considerable difficulty was also experienced in filling in the mast pond because of the soft nature of the ground.

The King Edward V11 class battleship "Hibernia" was to have been the first ship built on the new slip, but when she was due to be laid down, no lifting derricks had been fitted alongside. She was therefore laid down on the old No. 3 slip, which, with the new slip being numbered No. 3, became No. 4. By this time, the old No. 4 slip had become a Scrieve Board.

It was on 2 January, 1905 that the keel of "Minotaur" was laid down to become the first ship built on the new No. 3 slip. She was to be followed by "Temeraire" and "Collingwood". According to the two year limit for building armoured ships, the "Temeraire" should have been available to commission on 1 January, 1909 but in July, 1908 forty employees of the contractors working on the engines, Messrs. Hawthorn, Leslie and Co., Newcastle-on-Tyne, came out on strike and did not resume work until the end of September. This was one of the results of the engineers' strike in the north east of England, the Amalgamated Society of Engineers calling out their members engaged in the "Temeraire". This action delayed "Temeraire's" trials and meant that she did not commission until 15 May, 1909 to replace "Implacable" in the First Battle Squadron.

The date originally fixed for laying the keel of the "Collingwood" was 2 December, 1907, but to allow the firms to whom orders had been entrusted every opportunity for ensuring an uninterrupted supply of material when the Dockyard authorities were ready to build it into the ship, it was delayed until 3 February, 1908. The arrangements must have worked well, "Collingwood" being launched just nine months later.

After the launch of "Collingwood" and before the laying down of the next ship, "Invincible", the Admiralty decided to implement the original plan

Launch of H.M.S. TEMERAIRE 24th August 1907

that the slip could be lengthened when required. However, although extra foundations had been provided for up to 155 feet, the slip was only extended by 90 feet, all above the level of the Yard making the higher end about 10 feet above the roadway. The work was carried out by the Yard's own Works Department.

ROYAL VISIT IN 1902

Nothing before had provided greater popular interest and enthusiasm than the visit to Devonport in 1902 of Their Majesties King Edward VII and Queen Alexandra. The Queen named the battleship "Queen" at the second attempt, her first attempt at breaking the bottle of Colonial wine having failed. As that ship cleared the slipway, the King pressed a button to set in motion the machinery which, by means of a wire hawser, hauled a steel plate into position on the specially prepared fifteen sets of blocks which had been painted red, white and blue. The plate was decorated with four miniature Union Jacks, one at each corner. In a loud clear voice, His Majesty said "I declare the first keel-plate of the King Edward VII well and truly laid."

At the time, the slip was just large enough to

receive the "King Edward VII" although her bows would have reached the windows of the electrical shop. By the time the construction had reached that stage though, the workshop had been demolished and the machinery transferred to the new Machine Shop.

When the ship was launched His Majesty is said to have directed that she should always be employed as a Flagship, so it was ironic that she was to be mined and sunk in 1916 when there wasn't an Admiral on board.

A report from the Committee of Public Accounts, published in June, 1907 revealed that twelve months after the rudder casting for the "King Edward VII" was received and built into the ship, the Admiralty were informed by a dismissed employee of the Ayrshire Foundry Company, that on a Sunday, the Management had collected some workmen together and by means of electric welding had concealed a large fault in the casting. The Admiralty decided that the casting should be replaced. The firm denied that there was anything wrong but offered to replace the casting with a new one. This offer was accepted, but the second casting was full of flaws

Workmen going to work on H.M.S. KING EDWARD VII

and defects, and a third one proved no better. The Admiralty then decided that the casting should be made in the Dockyard and the cost charged to the contractors. The rumours of this particular transaction and the subsequent loss of other Admiralty orders brought such financial loss to the Ayrshire Foundry Company that it soon became bankrupt.

CHAPTER 12

THE KEYHAM EXTENSION —
THE GREATEST OF THEM ALL

For many years hope had been held out that Devonport Dockyard would be further extended. In December, 1859, Colonel Greene and a Mr. Wilberforce surveyed the land to the north of the Steam Yard at Keyham with a view to its development. In 1890 a scheme was produced which was to involve the expenditure of several million pounds, although to lessen the labour costs it was intended to use 1,500 convicts. The Lords of the Admiralty paid their official visit to Devonport when, it was hoped, they would give their blessing to the scheme. It was not to be though; it was again put off — but fortunately not for long.

The greatest extension that Devonport Dockyard had ever experienced was carried out under the provisions of the Naval Works Act of 1895 and was commenced without ceremony in February, 1896. About 3,400 men were employed and as a result of the employment of such a large number of men, a new residential district was created at Weston Mill.

At the southern end of the area of the extension scheme, outside the north basin of Keyham Yard, were berthed the "Vengeance" and "Indus". The first named had been built in Pembroke Dock in 1824, but for the last thirty years had been used at Keyham as a Receiving Hulk and afterwards as a Torpedo Store. When an attempt was made to tow her to the Cattewater for breaking up, the strain of the tugs was too much for the old timbers and she parted amidships and became embedded in the mud in two parts.

The effect of the extension was to double the combined areas of the Dockyard and Keyham Steam Yard, as then existing — adding about 113 acres of which 35 acres were situated above high water mark, being chiefly land that had been reclaimed from the Hamoaze by the dumping of rubble obtained from the rock excavated during the construction of Keyham Steam Yard. The rest of the area, 78 acres, was the foreshore of mud from High Water line to about Low Water of Spring Tides.

The extension provided for two basins — one tidal with an area of 10 acres and one closed of $35\frac{1}{2}$ acres. The closed basin was arranged with a direct entrance from the river and also with an alternative entrance lock, 730 feet long, which could also be used as a dry dock. Between the basins were constructed three graving docks originally numbered 4, 5 and 6 but later 8, 9 and 10. Two of them — Nos. 9 and 10 — 715 feet and 711 feet long respectively, could be entered from either end but No. 8, 480 feet long, from the closed basin only.

The lock and docks were each about 120 feet wide, and all entrances were provided with sliding caissons.

At least six contractors were asked to compete for this important undertaking but the Admiralty accepted the tender of Sir John Jackson, who had been contractor for part of the Manchester Ship Canal, and the contract was signed in January, 1896. The Civil Engineer-in-Chief of the Admiralty at the time was Major Sir Henry Pilkington, K.C.B., R.E., and the Superintendent Civil Engineer at Devonport was Mr., later Sir, Whatley Eliot, M.I.C.E.

For the exclusion of the tidal water from the site, a main cofferdam, 7,600 feet long, was constructed along the whole length of the river side of the proposed outer wall. Cross dams were also provided, connecting the main dam to the original foreshore at positions immediately north and south of the new graving docks and again at the extreme northern boundary of the extension. The piles in the main dam were of Oregon pine, 65 to 75 feet in length specially obtained from the United States. Sir John Jackson entered into a contract with the Pacific Pine Lumber Company for the necessary timber to be shipped from Port Blakeley, Washington. Many cargoes of pitch

The cofferdam around the extension

pine were also obtained from the Gulf of Mexico.

For the most part the cofferdam consisted of a double row of timber sheet piling which had an intervening space of five feet filled with puddled clay. The cofferdam itself took nearly two years to complete. Extensive damage was experienced during the progress of the work by the demolition of portions of the cofferdam during heavy gales.

The great problem to contend with in excavating the mud was that it was so soft that railway trucks could not be supported on it. For this reason, the mud over part of the site was excavated by means of a scoop, operated by cables which hauled it over the surface of the mud. Three discharge platforms — made to span over the cofferdam — were constructed with their shoreward ends splayed out in a fan-shape so that the mud scoops could be hauled up on to them and thence to a position over the barges where they were discharged. This scoop device, however, proved of limited use and as much as possible of the remainder of the material on the site of the new docks was removed by steam navvies loading into trains of tip wagons. These tip-wagons were, in turn, hauled up the incline on to the discharge staging.

The excavation of the large area of the Closed Basin was effected partly as before, by hauling these train loads up the inclined stagings, and partly by the use of two Lidgerwood cableways. The cableways each had a span of 1,520 feet and were arranged with two travelling tail-towers, 90 feet high, placed on railroads on the east side of the Closed Basin. Both these cableways converged to one head-tower, 100 feet high, fixed upon piles driven about 130 feet outside the main cofferdam. The skips traversing these cableways were filled by hand. The excavation of an area of approximately 80 acres to an average depth of 40 feet in the mud and ground overlaying the rock, and the removal of $1\frac{1}{4}$ million cubic yards of rock itself constituted an enormous task. It was recorded that over $4\frac{1}{4}$ million cubic yards of mud were removed from the site, and then taken in barges for disposal about 4 miles beyond Plymouth Breakwater. Six huge steel hoppers were especially built on the Clyde for transporting the mud out to sea.

The stone used for the docks was obtained

mainly from Cornwall—but supplemented with some from Norway — when it was found that the number of men employed in the Cornish quarries was not sufficient to produce the amount of material in time.

On an undertaking of this magnitude, where the various materials required are delivered in very large quantities, it was necessary to make extensive arrangements for landing, removing and storing them. Nearly all the materials were delivered by sea and to unload them two timber jetties were built on site. Four 10 ton steam cranes were kept constantly at work unloading ships. About 35,000 tons of various materials were landed each month, including 2,200 tons of Portland cement brought round (in sacks) from the Thames; 2,500 tons of granite, 1,500 tons of limestone from local quarries and 25,000 tons of shingle and sand. The last named was dredged up from the shore of Start Bay.

An enormous shed for the storage of cement and for the mixing of concrete was erected on the recreation ground used by the engineering students.

One of the greatest problems of the scheme was the construction of the main west and north walls of the closed basin. The great thickness of mud over most of the length of these walls would not permit trench excavation to be carried down to rock level. Use was made therefore of columns of pre-cast concrete sections, made to interlock one with another. Stacks of huge cast iron rings were loaded on these columns to force them down through the mud to the rock below. Up to 900 tons were used in some instances for compression. The columns, measuring 20 feet from front to back and 17 feet in width, were set out with ten feet spaces in between. These spaces were subsequently excavated to rock level and then completely filled with concrete. The tops of the columns were all finished at about 28 feet below cope level and the cope and quay were then completed in mass concrete with granite facing blocks above.

Numbers 9 and 10 docks were of the "double" type, in that by the use of an additional caisson at an intermediate stop they could be divided into two and each portion pumped out separately. These two docks, the lock and the tidal basin were handed over to the Admiralty early in 1906 but it was towards the end of that year before No. 8 was completed. This was because in August, 1906 the

Typical work area of the extension

Admiralty decided to lengthen it — to make it almost as long as the other two.

The "Hibernia" was the first ship docked in the Keyham Extension on 10 August, 1906. She left No. 1 Jetty in South Yard at 8.15 a.m. and was taken to the entrance to the Tidal Basin by three tugs and then hauled by wires into No. 9 Dock. The previous week the "Royal Sovereign" had entered the Tidal Basin, the first ship to do so, although the Basin had been completed some time previously but had not been used pending the deepening of the entrance.

This great undertaking — carried out over a period of ten years and costing £4,000,000 — was opened in February, 1907 when Their Royal Highnesses the Prince and Princess of Wales (who later became King George V and Queen Mary) sailed through the Lock into the closed basin on board "Vivid", the yacht of the Commander-in-Chief, Devonport.

This Royal Visit which should have been an event of great rejoicing amongst the local community, was not entirely so. Their Royal Highnesses had sailed up the Hamoaze from Admiralty House at Mount Wise, it being deemed "impracticable" for them to drive through the streets of Devonport. The civic authorities of that Borough, therefore, took no part in the opening of their Dockyard extension. Even the Mayor of Devonport declined his invitation, in protest at the way the arrangements had been handled. There was hardly a flag to be seen on shore.

Unfortunately, the weather was far from favourable. Yet there was complete absence of shelter of any kind, owing to the niggardliness of the Admiralty who appeared to have been so influenced by the taxpayer's demands for economy, that all the preparations for the opening of the Extension had to be carried out at a minimum cost.

The original intention was to use the new basin — which became known as the Prince of Wales's Basin - for ships in Reserve instead of having them moored in the Hamoaze. Towards completion though, it was decided to use it for fitting-out purposes so certain modifications were made including the construction of an additional pier or arm on the north side. Provision was also made, for the first time, for a complete H.P. air system to be made available at all the wharves and docksides.

Within two years of the completion of the Keyham Extension the Prince of Wales's Basin was dredged to increase its depth to 37 feet. It was also decided to again lengthen No. 8 Dock to make it long enough to admit the longest ship likely to be built within the next few years. In the first six months of 1910 it was lengthened 10 feet by cutting a triangular recess that would admit a ship's stem.

COAL WHARF

In 1891 the Admiralty had proposed that additional facilities for coaling warships should be provided at Keyham at a cost of £85,000. A pier with three jetties was to be constructed and preliminary borings to test the subsoil were carried out. However, commencement of the work was delayed and was subsequently overtaken by events. When mapping out the Keyham Extension, the Admiralty reserved at the north west corner of the area another site for a coaling station. It meant the removal to the other side of the Hamoaze of the signal station which was situated at that spot.

Work commenced in 1909 on what was to have been an electrically driven coaling depot that would surpass any in existence. Within twelve months, the work was sufficiently far advanced to permit the storage of coal. The plant was erected by Messrs. Fraser & Chalmers at a cost of £40,000.

CANTILEVER CRANE

In 1907, Messrs. Cowans, Sheldon & Co., Ltd., of Carlisle were commissioned to supply the heavy cranes for the new Extension — one 20 tons and two 30 tons steam travelling cranes; two 75 tons electric Fairbairn cranes; and one 160 tons electric revolving cantilever crane. The latter was to be sited on the east side of the Prince of Wales's Basin. To facilitate the work of raising and stepping this crane, three lattice-work wooden pillar supports were erected close to the crane's concrete foundation. The building of these supports, over fifty feet high and with a platform at the top, was carried out by Butters Bros. of Glasgow. On top of the main leg, or tower, a steam crane was fixed and at the base of each of the other two towers large quantities of iron ballast were deposited.

During tests in February, 1908, a steel forging which connected the top of the centre pillar of the crane to the two back stays, snapped at a point where there were two eye holes. As a result the pillar and back stays fell apart and the crane, with its boiler and fire box, crashed to the ground. Fortunately, the boiler did not explode. A portion of the machinery struck the side of the old gunnery ship "Cambridge" which was in the Basin being dismantled, but little damage was done beyond the smashing of her gangway. No personal injuries were sustained.

Completed in October, 1909, the first series of heavy weights the cantilever crane lifted in service were the fitting of the barbettes in "Collingwood". Its last working day was 9 September, 1978 after which it was dismantled, having been rendered redundant after the erection of a more modern crane on the east wall of No. 5 Basin.

"DEY" TIME CLOCK

For some time there were frequent disputes about the times of entry of men who had to start work in South Yard before the normal working hours and who left after the Yard Bell had been rung in the evening. The times of these men were kept by the Metropolitan Police at the main gate, and if a man happened to be just five minutes late the fact was duly recorded. When these records were compared with those kept by officials of the Yard, discrepancies were frequently discovered - resulting in some unpleasantness. To prevent any future doubt, a "Dey" time register clock, which would automatically record the times of entry and exit, was installed at the gate in July 1904. The Police welcomed this innovation as it would relieve them of a duty which was not altogether relished. For some time, the clock - which had been loaned to the Dockyard authorities by the owners - appeared to work satisfactorily, but within three months it was found that the number of "special men" was larger than the machine was capable of recording, so its use was discontinued.

REAR ADMIRAL W.H. HENDERSON'S INFLUENCE ON THE YARD

During his appointment to Devonport Yard (July 1902 to March, 1906) Rear Admiral W.H. Henderson introduced many reforms. On the whole, his innovations proved most successful and contributed much to the well-being of those employed in the Yard who were willing to put in a fair day's work. A few of his ideas though, were not well received, one of these relating to the regulations regarding the mid-day break of members of the writing staff. Those who had not sufficient time to reach their homes at mid-day had been in the habit of eating their meal in their offices. Admiral Henderson directed that they should not eat at their desks and, if necessary, they should be allowed a longer dinner time to enable them to make alternative arrangements. However, this order was soon rescinded.

The Admiral expressed his intention not to tolerate slackness or inefficiency in any man. Such men were to be reported to him by their departmental officers. As a result, several men were discharged for idling, or suspended for leaving their place of work before the ringing of the bell. At first his motive was not understood. Henderson realised that at the end of the financial year, 1903-04, a reduction of numbers in the Yard would be necessary and this could be done by "weeding out" the undesirables whose services would not be missed. Even established men were not secure. They were entitled to a pension on retirement but received a lower rate of pay than hired men; the difference in the pay being looked upon as deferred pay. The discharged established men had to go, though, without pension or gratuity of any kind.

Soon after he arrived, Henderson found that a large number of men and apprentices daily passed through the tunnel from one Yard to the other. Considering that a great deal of wasted time resulted from this, he decided to make use of "recorders" to check how much of this travelling was really necessary. It was claimed that, as a result of this check, for every seven men who had previously passed through the tunnel, only one did so afterwards.

To improve the means of communication between officers in the Yards, Admiral Henderson in October, 1904, introduced a Dockyard Postal Service, a man and two boys being detailed for the work.

Since January, 1849, to secure better co-operation between departments, it had been the custom for all officers to attend the office of the

Admiral Superintendent at 9.30 each morning for "readings" - the reading by the A.S. or his representative of all orders and communications received from the Admiralty during the previous 24 hours. In January, 1906 Admiral Henderson abolished this daily event and replaced it with a weekly gathering of Principal Officers on Tuesday mornings.

Other notable improvements which were introduced on the initiative of Admiral Henderson were:—

(a) the transport by boat of working parties. The harbour was mapped out into sections, and steamboats bearing distinctive numbers proceeded at regular intervals from the principal landing steps, calling at the various ships en route. Long wooden stages were moored alongside the Dockyard to facilitate embarkation;

(b) a regular 20 minute train service between the Yards. Previously the service was slow and uncertain resulting in large numbers of officers and men standing about waiting for a train;

(c) using travelling cranes to transport lengths of cable between ships and store, replacing teams of horses which dragged the cables along the roads;

(d) the system whereby a continuous and regular supply of materials and stores was made more readily available to ships refitting. A special party of "providers" and the erection of "ready use stores" near the centres of work obviated the need for detaching men to obtain articles from the central stores; and

(e) making special arrangements to place all vessels requiring large repairs in either a dock or a basin instead of leaving them moored in the stream, thus cutting out boat transport.

Efficiency had been the aim of Admiral Henderson, and in securing this he had had to deal drastically with old prejudices and customs. However, by the end of his appointment the Dockyard had never been in a higher state of efficiency or been more capable of meeting the demands made on its resources.

Yet, curiously enough, it was during the regime of this distinguished officer that an event occurred in Devonport Yard which caused a definite change in Admiralty policy. The Yard was building the second class protected cruiser "Encounter" but as there was no urgency for her completion, she was being treated as a 'stand-by' job. Launched in 1902 she was not ready for her trials until 1905. Her machinery had been built in the Yard, but when it came to fitting her boilers, it was discovered that an extraordinary miscalculation had been made and that they were too big to fit into the space allotted. Considerable expense and loss of time resulted, although when the "Encounter" was eventually completed she proved a very successful ship and had a long career of useful service.

As a direct consequence of this experience the Admiralty decided that no more machinery should be built in the Royal Dockyards. The "Encounter" affair was cited in the argument that private contract firms could build machinery better and cheaper than the Dockyards.

SIGNAL STATIONS

On 6 June, 1906 - the same day as the launch of "Minotaur" - a new Dockyard signal station in North Yard was completed. It was quite an imposing building, situated near the Flagstaff Steps, commanding an uninterrupted view of the whole harbour. The building was three storeys high, yet it had been built and equipped within six months. It provided accommodation for the Flag Captain and his staff, replacing their offices which had previously been at the entrance to Keyham Steam Yard.

Three years later a signal station was also built in South Yard on a site formerly occupied by the Waiting Room used by officers and men waiting for boat transport to their ships in the Hamoaze. It was approached from the river by a flight of stone steps close to the entrance to No. 2 Dock. When completed in November, 1909, it formed another link in the chain of signal stations extending from Mount Wise to the extreme north end of the Yard at Weston Mill Lake.

OTHER BUILDINGS

Although, obviously, most attention was directed towards the vast undertaking of the Keyham Extension, other building work was also being carried out in other parts of the Yard. In

August, 1901 it was decided to build a new Telephone Exchange at Keyham to replace a system which was most unsatisfactory, it often being quicker to send a messenger than phone.

In the programme for 1902-03, £1,800 was allocated for the erection of a new Surgery. It was to be erected on a site between the Metropolitan Police offices and the Dockyard School in South Yard. When completed, the old surgery at the end of the Terrace was used as offices for the Works Department. In August, 1912 another new Surgery was opened in North Yard.

In 1903 a Drawing Office was erected for the Chief Engineer's Department at Keyham. Built on the descending roadway inside the main gate, its 200 feet frontage had grey limestone facings and Portland stone dressings. It cost about £9,000 and took 15 months to complete, the work being carried out by Messrs. A.R. Lethbridge & Sons of Plymouth.

This period also saw the erection of new machine shops adapted to the class of work for which the new building slip would be available. These included a Shipwrights' Machine Shop, a Shipfitting Shop, and a Plumbers' Shop.

A lofty and spacious building, 125ft. x 50ft. x 45ft., was erected by Messrs. Lysaght of Bristol, near the Camber in South Yard, to provide accommodation for the repair of large buoys. The building's great height and breadth was necessary to enable the free movement of the powerful travelling crane used for transporting the buoys. The difficulty of providing suitable doors for the lofty entrance was overcome by fitting a roller screen, with vertical movement. It could be moved up or down by just two men.

Another notable building completed in 1908 was the Whitehead Torpedo Store, near the North Gate of the Dockyard. Two storeys high, built of brick with stone facings, the principal dimensions were 300 feet x 103 feet x 75 feet high. The foundations had been laid, under Sir John Jackson's directions, three years earlier but were allowed to settle before building operations continued. The ground floor provided space, in racks, for 800 torpedoes, whilst on the upper floor were the offices, workrooms, testing and parting rooms.

Other buildings included Gun Mounting Stores and workshops, which occupied a straight line facing the Prince of Wales's Basin; and a Rigging House and Mast House in close proximity to the Tidal Basin.

CENTRAL OFFICES

However, the most imposing buildings built soon after the opening of the Keyham Extension were the aptly named Central Offices.. In 1903, the Civil Lord of the Admiralty had visited a proposed office site at Keyham - almost at the centre of the Dockyard between Mutton Cove and the north end of the Extension. At the time the various offices were scattered over South Yard and the idea was to bring all the principal offices into one building. It was anticipated these new offices would cost about £100,000 but the tendency in official quarters was to economise and the project was shelved.

However, in March, 1909, the Admiralty accepted the tender of Mr. Carkeek of Redruth, and the work was taken in hand almost immediately. By October, 1911, the new offices were ready for occupation. The Electrical Engineer and his staff were the first to move in, followed by the Captain of the Dockyard and the Engineering Manager. The transfer of the Admiral Superintendent and Constructive Manager's Department though was deferred until after the launch of "Centurion" in November, 1911.

The ground floor of the Admiral Superintendent's former office at the end of the Terrace was then taken over by the Constructor in charge of the building slips, although the first floor was retained as an Admiral's Board Room for use in an emergency.

CHAPTER 13
THE TWENTIETH CENTURY

During the early years of the twentieth century, as the sizes of warships were increasing, so Devonport's docking facilities were becoming overstrained and, at times, unable to cope with the requirement.

In October, 1904, the "King Edward V11", more than twelve months after her launch, had to be sent to Portsmouth to be docked for the removal of her launching gear; for the simple reason that there was no dock at Devonport big enough to take her.

In 1905, the crisis became acute when the "Caesar" had, for six weeks, been occupying the only available dock whilst "Hannibal", "Prince George" and "Royal Sovereign" were all waiting to be docked. The Admiral Superintendent was already pressing Sir John Jackson to let him know the earliest date when a dock in the new Extension would be available for "Hibernia" which had left the slip on 17 June, 1905.

The gates at the entrance to the North Dock in South Yard, having been in service for many years and not repaired since 1874, were condemned in May, 1906. They were made of wood, and required a lot of manual labour to open them - forty men on each side to work the capstans. A concrete dam was built across the entrance by the S.C.E. Department, whilst new gates were built within the dock by the C.M. Department. The new gates were completed and the dam removed in February, 1909. Then work commenced on widening and lengthening the dock to double its capacity for docking destroyers. The length of the dock was increased by ten feet along its centre line and, with a well-proportioned curve near the head, allowed two "River" class destroyers to be docked at one time.

In May, 1906, alterations were proposed to Nos. 6 and 7 docks at Keyham to also make them more suitable for destroyers. Widening the floor of the docks by the removal of the lower stone steps or altars, would allow the docking of the larger destroyers in groups of three instead of two - one being taken in stern first and the other two bows first as normal.

The other dock, No. 5, at Keyham had become known as the Submarine Dock, its close proximity to the Electrical Fitting Shop making it especially suitable for this type of vessel. In November, 1907, it was taxed to its limit with five submarines - four 'B' class and one 'A' - undergoing refit and examination in it. The need to protect these vessels whilst refitting was felt particularly at that time of year. Canvas coverings were used and although it was proposed to provide a permanent roof over this dock, it was never carried out.

JETTY FACILITIES

A great lack of jetty facilities was also revealed. In January, 1900 in order to dock the cruiser "Blake" it was necessary to remove "Implacable" into the stream because where she was berthed

alongside, her bows were blocking the entrance to No. 2 Dock.

To improve the approaches to wharves and docks in South Yard, and to make them available to the deepest draught vessels, dredging - and blasting - operations were carried out off No. 1 Jetty and off the entrance to No. 2 dock. The presence of a rubble shoal off No. 2 Dock had long been a source of anxiety. When "Niobe's" undocking date was delayed for a couple of days the state of the tide caused it to be put off for a full week. The highest tide would only give her a few inches clearance and the Yard decided not to risk it. The danger was removed in November, 1900, though, when Messrs. Hill and Company, who had been employed on dredging operations at the entrance to the Hamoaze, moved their diving bell and steam drill "Epsilon" to the dock entrance to commence clearance operations.

Between 1905-08 an additional jetty was built to the southward of the new No. 3 slip by filling in the rest of the Mast Pond. It was to be primarily used by vessels arriving with stores for new construction work.

In 1908, to facilitate berthing and to make the best possible use of the space available along the sea wall, it was divided into suitable lengths, thereby creating "wharves".

NEW SHALLOW DOCK

In 1895, it had been suggested that the two building slips at the Mutton Cove end of the Yard be converted into one. The Admiralty directed that measurements be taken and estimates made of the cost and time required. Three years passed and nothing had been done, so when it was proposed to build the new No. 3 slip, it was thought it would mean the destruction of Nos. 1 and 2 slips. The fear proved unfounded so tenders were invited to convert the two building sheds into an open slipway. Still nothing was done though, and the slips fell into disuse.

Then, in August 1909, it was proposed to convert them both into shallow docks each capable of receiving two or more torpedo craft. At the time about 60 destroyers and torpedo boats were based at Devonport. Sometimes six of them at a time were docked in the Lock in North Yard.

Three months later a decision was made that the development at Mutton Cove would not be so extensive as first planned. No. 1 slip, and roof over it, was to be retained, but the roof over No. 2 was to be removed and the building slip converted to a dock capable of taking shallow draught vessels.

A concrete cofferdam was built across the entrance to enable work to be carried out. The Shallow Dock, as it became known, was completed at a cost of £40,000. With parallel sides throughout its length and being square at the head, it was a departure from the old established shape.

The new dock was first used in April, 1912 when the torpedo boats Nos. 99 and 107 were docked there. In June, 1907, T.B.99 had foundered off Berry Head after her main shaft had broken and pierced her bottom plating. All the crew were saved and taken on board the torpedo gunboat "Dryad". Devonport Dockyard workers were sent to salvage her, and she was lifted in two parts and taken into Elbury Cove, near Brixham. From there, she was brought to Devonport and in December, both parts of her were placed in No. 4 Dock, South Yard. After her damaged plating had been renewed and both sections joined up, T.B.99 was able to continue in service until 1920.

CANTEEN AND RESTAURANT ASSOCIATIONS

In 1898 it had been proposed that the workmen in the Yard should establish a canteen, controlled by themselves, simply for the purpose of supplying meals to the men who were unable to get to their homes at mid-day. The proposal was favourably received by the Admiralty and a canvass of the men showed that they too were unanimously in favour of it. The Admiralty asked the Admiral Superintendent to furnish the necessary plans, with the estimated cost and time to complete, for a canteen in South Yard, where all the cooking would be done, with a "branch" at Keyham. Correspondence passed between the Yard and the Admiralty for years though, before it was finally decided to build three Dining Halls, one in South Yard over the Saw Mill, one at Keyham, and one in the new North Yard. To control these Halls, the Devonport Dockyard Workmen's Canteen and Restaurant Association was formed. The Admiral Superintendent performed the opening ceremony of the main Hall in North Yard in September, 1913. The Hall was capable of seating over 1,500 men and served a good meal - meat, two vegetables, and a pudding -

for 5d. The Association proved a most useful and profitable undertaking. During the 1914-18 war, when troops embarked or disembarked at the Dockyard, the canteens came to their aid, and the soldiers' wives and children were provided with a hot meal free of charge. In 1932, the trading account for the Canteens showed a loss for the first time since their inception. This was attributed to the fact that the clocking-in system at their place of work had obviated the need for the workmen to attend the muster stations which were sited near the canteens.

NO. 5 SLIP "CONVERSION"

After the cruiser "Encounter" had been built and launched from No. 5 slip in 1902, the slip fell into disuse. In 1910 work was taken in hand to convert it and make it suitable for boat repair. A new floor was fitted and massive hauling-up rings were fixed into concrete beds. It provided accommodation for a double line of large boats, which were hauled up the slipway with the aid of 20 h.p. electrically driven winches.

Two years later though, it was again used for ship-building. An oil-carrier for the Royal Fleet Auxiliary - to be named "Carol" - was laid down on 14 November 1912 and after her launch in July, 1913 another oiler, "Ferol", was laid down. The latter was the first ship built at Devonport with internal combustion engines, these being supplied by Fairfield Shipbuilding and Engineering Co., Ltd., Glasgow.

ADVENT OF THE BATTLECRUISER

The laying down of the "Indefatigable" on 25 February, 1909 was a significant advance in the building of cruisers at Devonport for, up to that time, she was by far the largest and most powerful cruiser built in the Yard. So much indeed was the advance that even the classification had changed from "First Class Protected cruiser" for the "Minotaur" to "Battlecruiser" for "Indefatigable".

During the last few years it had been customary to fix launching ceremonies for Saturday afternoons, thus avoiding the necessity to close the Yard during ordinary working hours. On the occasion of the launch of "Indefatigable" though, the state of the tide rendered a Thursday launch inevitable. The Yard was closed on the afternoon of that day but the men were given the opportunity of working to make up the lost time!

H.M.S. MARLBOROUGH in Plymouth Sound

LAST OF THE COAL BURNING BATTLESHIPS

One of the last of the coal-burning British battleships, was laid down in the Yard on 25 January, 1912. The ceremony was semi-private, invitations only having been sent to naval officers, dockyard officials and their wives. The name of this new vessel was not displayed as it was still awaiting the Royal approval. When launched on 24 October, 1912 she was named "Marlborough".

That same day the keel plate of the "Aurora" was laid down on an adjoining slip. This class of cruiser - the "Arethusa" class light cruisers - comprised the first vessels of the type in the R.N. to be entirely oil-fired. To assist the artisans in the east end of London, the Admiralty placed the order for "Aurora's" machinery with the Thames Iron Works but owing to financial difficulties this decision had to be rescinded and the machinery was finally ordered from the Parsons Marine Steam Turbine Co., Ltd., Wallsend-on-Tyne.

DEVONPORT'S MOST FAMOUS WARSHIP

The most famous warship ever to leave the slipways of Devonport Yard was the "Warspite" - a Queen Elizabeth class battleship, the second ship of the first group of ships in the R.N. to be wholly oil-fired and to mount 15" guns. She was launched on 26 November, 1913 and saw service in both World Wars.

"Warspite" was badly damaged at the Battle of Jutland in 1916, but was with the combined Allied Fleet in the North Sea at the surrender of the German High Seas Fleet on 21 November, 1918.

Early on the morning of 13 April, 1940, accompanied by nine destroyers, she steamed up the Ofot Fjord to Narvik in Norway and in these confined waters, eight enemy destroyers were sunk and German shore batteries heavily bombarded. In March, 1941 she took part in the Battle of Matapan, when she damaged two Italian cruisers. The last major operations of her illustrious career took place in June, 1944 when she carried out bombarding duties off Normandy;

H.M.S. WARSPITE in dock

and in November, 1944 when she supported the landings at Walcheren.

"Warspite" did not escape these World War 2 operations unscathed. A bomb damaged her port side when off Crete in May, 1941; whilst bombarding Salerno in September, 1943 she was hit by two radio-controlled bombs; and on 13 June, 1944 whilst on passage from Portsmouth to Rosyth she was damaged by a mine.

She was defiant to the end. After being stripped at Portsmouth, she was being towed to the Clyde to be broken up when, in the Channel on 20 January, 1947, the tow parted. For three days she drifted, until being driven ashore in Prussia Cove, Cornwall. In 1950 she was floated across Mount's Bay and beached again off Marazion. The work of breaking her up continued until 1956.

CHAPTER 14

OUTBREAK OF WAR

In September, 1914 Rear Admiral Sir Christopher Cradock was appointed to the command of the fleet in the South Atlantic. In pursuance of Admiralty orders he proceeded with his ships into the South Pacific to search for the German fleet under Admiral Von Spee. Off Coronel, on the coast of Chile, the two fleets made contact and although inferior in fire power and speed, Cradock accepted the challenge. During the ensuing battle, his flagship "Good Hope", and the "Monmouth" were both sunk with heavy loss of life.

Winston Churchill, then First Lord of the Admiralty, decided to send the battlecruisers "Inflexible" and "Invincible" as reinforcements. The ships would have to pass through the Tropics and keep at sea for a long period, so it was essential that if the ships' equipment was to be made efficient, their coal supplies adequate, and the ships' companies fit, certain alterations would have to be made. The ships therefore were directed to Devonport Dockyard, where the men worked feverishly day and night to get them ready for sea. On Monday, 9 November, 1914 Admiral Godfrey Munday, the Admiral Superintendent, told the Admiralty that the earliest date for completion of the work was midnight on the 13th. However, Churchill said they were to be ready to sail on Wednesday, the 11th - "if necessary, Dockyardmen should be sent away with the ships, to return as opportunity may offer". And that is exactly what happened.

Admiral F.C. Doveton Sturdee flew his flag in "Invincible" and on 27 November assumed command of the entire force which included the Devonport manned cruisers "Cornwall" and "Carnarvon", and the "Kent", "Bristol" and "Glasgow".

The ensuing battle was this country's one really decisive naval victory of the First World War. Von Spee's flagship, "Scharnhorst", and her sister ship, "Gneisenau", put up a great fight but were overwhelmed. The only enemy ship to escape was the cruiser "Dresden", which fled back in to the Pacific, but she, too, was later dealt with at Juan Fernandez.

Within a week of the departure of "Inflexible" and "Invincible", the "Royal Oak" was launched from South Yard. She took to the water on 17 November, 1914, before a large number of specially invited guests, but owing to the war, the general public were not admitted. In case supplies of oil fuel became limited in time of war, the "Royal Oak" was originally designed to burn coal but during construction, an "all fuel oil" policy was adopted. She proved to be the last battleship built at Devonport.

A "Royal Sovereign" class battleship, "Resistance", was included in the 1914-15 programme for ship construction at Devonport but work on her was never commenced. On the declaration of war, work on warships that could not be completed within six months was suspended. Optimistically it was thought that the war would end within six months.

Concurrently with the building of the "Royal Oak" on No. 3 slip and the "Ferol" on No. 5 slip, the cruiser "Cleopatra" was built on No. 4 slip.

These surface ships were followed by the construction of the first locally built submarines. These vessels J5 and J6, were laid down on 26

April, 1915 on No. 5 slip which was still covered, thereby screening the submarines from view. They were launched within five months, in the presence of Their Majesties King George V and Queen Mary. Immediately prior to the launching, Their Majesties had watched the bending of the first frame, after it had been drawn hot from a furnace, for one of the next pair of submarines to be built. Earlier in the afternoon, they had toured North Yard, visiting the "Royal Oak" then being fitted out in No. 8 dock.

Three more submarines were built on the same slipway during the First World War - K6 and K7 launched 31 May, 1916; and J7 launched 21 February, 1917. The K class submarines were, except for experiments in "Swordfish" in 1916-17, the first R.N. submarines to use steam-power for propulsion. The idea resulted from the need for submarines which could maintain their station with the Grand Fleet when cruising. The K boats surpassed all previous designs both in size and speed - 24 knots on the surface and 9 knots submerged. Underwater the submarine was propelled by electric power. For the submarine to submerge, the funnels were hinged down and lowered into the superstructure, the funnel openings closing simultaneously by means of a watertight cover operated by a motor from the turbine room. An additional valve was fitted on the hull at the base of the funnel uptakes. Watertight covers for air vents in the boiler room were hydraulically operated from that room. However, steam propelled submarines were not a success.

The first time K6 submerged in the basin of the Yard, she refused to surface. The Inspector of Engine Fitters, Mr. L. Selley, traced the fault and made temporary repairs. After an anxious two hours, the submarine rose to the surface. The incident caused such consternation amongst the Dockyard workers that several of them refused to dive in her the second time. In April, 1919, Mr. Selley was presented with the O.B.E. by the Lord Lieutenant of Devon.

The cruiser "Frobisher" was also laid down during the war, on 2 August, 1916 when the keel plate was laid by Lady Maud Warrender, the wife of the Commander-in-Chief, Plymouth. This class of ship was designed to operate in the Atlantic and as it was thought oil fuel might not be obtainable in distant parts, they were planned with some coal

capacity and four small coal-burning boilers that would provide sufficient steam for cruising speed. However, after the Armistice in 1918 work on the ship was delayed and she became practically a 'stand-by' ship for the workmen. She was therefore in hand for a longer period than any other modern warship - the original coal/oil concept was no longer deemed necessary and she was completed as an oil-burner.

SPECIAL WAR-WORK

In additional to the work of new construction, the war caused an enormous amount of other work, more or less of a special character, which in the aggregate tested the full capacity of the Dockyard. The docking and fitting out, often at short notice, of large numbers of H.M. Ships of all classes and other vessels for war service; periodical refits of those ships; carrying out heavy repairs to war - and merchant ships which had been damaged in action or collision; fitting out minelayers, minesweepers and Q ships - a formidable list on which the work proceeded concurrently and continuously. The large number of vessels in the docks and basins at any one time bore testimony to the extent of the work in hand.

In carrying out the work, full advantage was taken of the use of mechanical labour saving appliances, such as portable pneumatic tools for drilling, riveting and caulking. Similarly electric welding, introduced in 1915, was extensively used in lieu of structural riveting. Much excellent service was also rendered by oxy-acetylene welding plants. In 1905 this process of cutting and welding metal was in the experimental stage, but its easy portable nature made it ideal for quickly removing large portions of damaged hull plating.

About 20,000 were employed in the Yard during the war; obviously mostly men, but many women were also employed at that time.

Q SHIPS

Plymouth was a centre of operations against German U-boats, operations being carried out by a variety of vessels, assisted by airships, seaplanes and kite balloons. The most famous amongst the vessels though, were the Q ships. They were originally known as "Decoy Ships" but when towards the end of 1916 the Admiralty identified them as Q1, Q2, Q3, etc. they became popularly known as Q ships.

Many of them were fitted out at Devonport, manned by gallant officers and men who added so many glorious chapters to Britain's naval history by their daring adventures and thrilling achievements. These ships looked like innocent merchant ships - which they had been before being fitted with hidden weapons. They operated alone, which enticed submarines to attack them. Unwanted personnel - the 'panic party' - would take to the boats, but when the submarine came in range, guns' crews left on board the Q ship would uncover concealed weapons and engage the enemy.

One of the most famous Q ship commanders, Gordon Campbell, fitted out his ships at Devonport. On 21 October, 1915 he commissioned the tramp steamer "Loderer" as a Decoy Ship. On passage to Queenstown her name was changed to "Farnborough", which led to a rumour that the "Loderer" had been sunk. In this ship - which eventually became Q5 - he sank U68 and U83; in "Pargust" (ex-"Vittoria") he sank UC29; and in "Dunraven" another submarine was possibly damaged. All three ships were awarded Victoria Crosses. In Q5 Gordon Campbell himself gained his V.C., but in the other two ships they were drawn for and were awarded to one officer and one rating from each ship.

After the Armistice, local people were able to inspect a Q ship and two U-boats. The "Hyderabad" was berthed in Millbay Docks and 3,000 people visited her, a small charge being made in aid of naval charities. She was afterwards moved to the Dockyard before going on to Torquay in December, 1918. The two U-boats on view were the U126 - which had had a particularly bad war record - and U161, which had never been in commission.

COLD STORE IN NORTH YARD

One of Devonport's most well known harbour-side buildings, the Cold Store depot, was built during the war at a cost of £53,000. With a storage capacity of 5,000 tons of meat, it was erected for the Ministry of Food, but when the war ended they no longer required it, so it was taken over by the Admiralty as part of the Victualling Department facilities.

DEVONPORT'S ONLY DESTROYER

It was originally planned that the modified "W" class destroyer "Watson" should be built at the Govan Yard of Fairfield Shipbuilding and Engineering Co., Ltd., but on 26 November, 1918 the contract was transferred to Devonport. The "Watson" would have been Devonport Dockyard's one and only destroyer but she was destined never to be completed.

When construction was well advanced towards launching, work on her stopped. In September, 1919, men began taking her to pieces; she was cut up on the slipway and the material used for other purposes.

CHAPTER 15

BETWEEN THE WARS

The termination of hostilities in 1918 aroused much apprehension over the future of the Yard. Large overtime earnings could not be expected to continue and there was fear of considerable reductions in numbers employed. The men though were assured that there was enough work in the Yard for at least two years.

In spite of the uncertainty prevailing, in July, 1919 the Unions called for a vote amongst their members — for or against strike action — if the government didn't agree to pay the same wages as private firms. For example, Admiralty engineers received 39/- a week, but the pay for those with private firms ranged from 43/10½d. to 48/-. The Admiralty claimed that opportunities afforded their employees for establishment with pension rights and greater regularity of employment off-set any disadvantages in pay. A ballot was held amongst the men — the shipwrights even had a vote first on whether to have the ballot — in which they were asked to decide whether (a) to strike; (b) to go to arbitration; or (c) to accept the 2/- a week increase offered by the Admiralty. An over-whelming majority — about 10 to 1 — were in favour of arbitration.

With a view to relieving the unemployment problem in Plymouth and Devonport, the Local Advisory Committee put forward various suggestions on how the Government could help. This resulted in Dr. Macnamara, Parliamentary Secretary to the Admiralty, receiving a deputation from all the Dockyard towns. They wished to obtain some definite information on the future of the Dockyards and to make some suggestions for employing the men who were drawing unemployment benefit in order to tide themselves over the difficult period until the launching of municipal schemes absorbed surplus local labour. They pointed out that it would be unwise to build a large number of workmen's houses in Dockyard towns if there were to be heavy reductions in the Yards. They urged that if Government work was not sufficient to maintain the full strength of workmen, the surplus labour should be utilised in making good the loss in merchant shipping. Dr. Macnamara assured the deputations that it was the intense desire of the Admiralty to reduce to a minimum any changes that would bring distress, but he frankly admitted that discharges must take place. At the time there was plenty of work repairing ships that had been somewhat neglected during the war, but few, if any, new ships would be required. When the repair work was completed, gradual discharges would be inevitable. With regard to the proposed use of the Yards for mercantile shipbuilding, he said the Admiralty were giving it serious consideration.

However, on the last Saturday of September, 1919, 1,500 men received a fortnight's notice. On the Sunday morning though, the Admiral Superintendent received instructions to suspend the notices. It was assumed that this was to prevent the numbers of men on strike from the railway industry at the time being augmented by men being discharged from the Yards.

About two weeks later, another deputation, this time from the Port Development Committee of Plymouth Town Council, called on the First Lord of the Admiralty (Mr. Walter Long) pressing for the adoption of merchant shipbuilding in Devonport Dockyard and for the use of its North Yard for commercial purposes. They pointed out that "at the outbreak of war in 1914, about 14,000 were employed in the Yard and this number grew to over 20,000 during hostilities. Now only 16,000 are employed and further discharges are foreshadowed."

The First Lord reassured the deputation that he could not at present foresee the numbers reducing to below the pre-war standard. It was pointed out by him though, that the number of men being discharged could be reduced by either

(a) bringing forward work on H.M. Ships — which unfortunately would bring only temporary relief to unemployment; or

(b) adopting a short time system, i.e. one day less per week.

If scheme (b) was agreed, he intimated that the notices of discharges would be withdrawn. A ballot amongst the men resulted as follows:—

For closing one day: 5,875; against: 2,628
For closing pm Friday and am Saturday: 5,601
For closing Mondays: 274

Nearly 9,000 men though abstained from voting.

Some months later the Industrial Section of all Government workers decided against the scheme for short time working, on the grounds that wages in their establishments were already so low that any reduction would bring earnings below the poverty line.

In spite of this opposition, the Cabinet decided to reduce the working week by seven hours, commencing 23 January, 1921. The benefit of short-time working was made apparent when in the first week, 150 unemployed workmen were entered into the Yard, and a similar number every day for the next ten days.

Although it continued to be a bone of contention, opposition to short-time working gradually waned. It seemed that the Trade Unions had made their protest and then allowed matters to stand. However, in August, 1921 it was decided to revert — in stages — to full working hours; first of all to 42 hours and then on 26 September, to 47 hours including Saturday morning.

THE COLWYN COMMITTEE

In 1919, a Committee of eighteen persons, including Lovell R. Dunstan, Mayor of Plymouth, was appointed by the Admiralty under the Chairmanship of Lord Colwyn, to consider the future use of the Dockyards.

Their terms of reference were:—

To consider how far it may be possible to utilise

any facilities which the Admiralty may have available for the construction of merchant ships of any kind, either

    (a) by investigating offers of private shipbuilders to lease such facilities and offer employment to Admiralty employees; or

    (b) by considering offers from firms desirous of placing orders for new merchant tonnage to be constructed by the Dockyards.

The Committee, it was added, would also investigate any proposals for the use of any part of Admiralty dock accommodation for commercial purposes.

Their report, which was completed in December, 1919, but not made public until three months later, considered it was not possible to carry out the suggestions that portions of the Dockyards should be leased to private shipbuilders. They suggested though that the Admiralty might undertake the building of merchant ships, though they did not regard this as a permanent solution to the difficulty.

The most important recommendation from Devonport's point of view was that the Yard should be used as a terminal port. During a visit to Plymouth in April, 1920, Mr. Walter Long, First Lord of the Admiralty, stated that the Board were prepared to hand over to the local Corporation the west arm of the Prince of Wales's Basin for the purpose. The Colwyn Committee acknowledged that the scheme would present some difficulties, but they did not consider them insuperable. "This is a national emergency during the continuance of which it is the duty of the Admiralty to provide work in the Dockyard towns for the men whom they collected into their service, and retained, during the war."

It must be borne in mind that the Dockyard towns depended almost entirely upon the Navy for their existence, and that Admiralty policy in the past had tended to discourage any extension of the ports on commercial lines which might otherwise have taken place. It followed therefore, that these towns had no immediate means of filling the gap caused by the decline in Admiralty expenditure. Furthermore, the general housing situation throughout the country made it impossible for large numbers of men to be transferred elsewhere.

The Committee carefully considered the offers put forward by private shipbuilders to lease portions of the Dockyards, but they came unanimously to the conclusion that in no Dockyard had any such scheme any likelihood of commercial success. The layout and organisation of the Yards did not lend themselves to subdivision. There was one source of power (of all kinds) in each Yard and one set of shops to supply both new construction and repair. Dual control of these essentials would be an unworkable proposition, and a commercial firm would require a priority of user which the Navy could not always afford. This would have required considerable alterations, and perhaps additions, to the power services and workshops. "There would also be a fruitful source of discontent between the two bodies of men in disparity of wages and conditions of employment" they added.

They examined the possibility of the Dockyards undertaking mercantile shipbuilding under Admiralty control. Before the War the building of warships was carried out on lines that would be totally different from those that would be necessary for the construction of merchant ships to be a commercial success. Rapidity of delivery and economy of construction were not usually the guiding factors. New construction was occasionally delayed by the urgency of repairs to commissioned ships; alterations in design were continually occurring; and there were consequent periods in which work was proceeding at a rate far below the possible output; and, as in all Government Departments, the machinery of control was far more elaborate and counted for more than in a private undertaking which had sufficient protection in its profit and loss account. Moreover, there were important differences between merchant ship and warship building. "We consider, therefore, that if merchant shipbuilding is to be undertaken certain changes in organisation and procedure are essential."

"If the matter is taken up wholeheartedly though, we recommend that the Admiralty should utilize their surplus facilities in the construction of merchant vessels. The concentration on these vessels by the building Yards would release sufficient repair and reconditioning work to keep the other Dockyards in employment."

"We consider that this proposal offers to the Admiralty an expedient for tiding over a difficult period of distress, and the Committee hope and expect that in the present position of shipping trade, the Admiralty will be able to build without loss."

One of the proposals of the Colwyn Committee, which was insisted upon by the Admiralty, was that the rules of demarcation should be waived in the event of mercantile shipbuilding being undertaken in Royal Dockyards. For some weeks the shipwrights at Devonport were a stumbling block to any agreement between the various trades. They considered their long-worked-for privileges were endangered and there was a large vote by them against the proposals when a ballot was taken. Two weeks later though, the Amalgamated Union of the three principal trades accepted the proposals of the Colwyn Committee, the shipwrights then saying "they had no wish to frustrate the objects aimed at, and agreed upon, by other trades."

MERCHANT SHIPBUILDING

In October, 1919, Messrs. J. & H. Maxwell Jones of Plymouth had offered to place an order for Devonport Dockyard to build a coasting steamer of nearly 1,000 tons deadweight, and a steam trawler. The following month, Messrs Cayser Irvine and Co. offered to order the construction of two merchant steamers, but the Admiralty informed both firms that they were then unable to accept.

In February, 1920 a Swansea shipowner offered to order two hulls of ships about 250 feet long for which machinery was available, but this, too, was not acceptable as machinery work was wanted in the Dockyard as well as hull work. There were also unaccepted offers from the Cunard Steamship Company to recondition the liners "Caronia" and "Saxonia".

Within a couple of months though, the building of merchant ships did commence in the Yard. Two were laid down for private owners — a standard steamer of 5,150 tons deadweight for Messrs. J. & H. Maxwell Jones and a small collier for the Plymouth Co-operative Society.

A Royal Fleet Auxiliary oiler was then provided for in the 1920 estimates "in accordance with the Colwyn Committee's recommendation". The machinery for her, and her sister ship being built at Pembroke, was constructed in the Royal Dockyards too, different parts being allocated to Devonport, Portsmouth and Chatham in order to provide work for the Engineering Departments. The ship at Devonport was laid down as Merchant No. 1 without ceremony on 14 June 1920 and was launched 21 June, 1921 after being named "Olna" by Mrs. Underhill, wife of the Admiral Superintendent.

The contract for a second oiler — a fixed price contract — was signed in August, 1920, to build the "Nassa" for the Anglo-Saxon Petroleum Co. Ltd., of London. This 5,680 tons vessel was laid down on 8 March, 1921 and launched 28 March, 1922.

A VARIETY OF OTHER UNUSUAL JOBS

To ease the discharge problems, a variety of unusual jobs were carried out at Devonport, and additional work was obtained by transferring partially built ships from other Yards. For example:—

(a) several large transports, which had finished their wartime role for the Government, were refitted;

(b) the Australian steamer "Nairana", which had been used as a seaplane carrier, was taken in hand for reconstruction, preparatory to her return to commercial service. She was in the Yard for over twelve months before being handed over to her owners on Saturday, 29th January, 1921 and sailing to Australia the next day;

(c) the refitting of the liner "Cap Polonia", the finest of the German liners acquired by Great Britain — an important job which lasted for several months;

(d) 24 American submarine chasers were docked for overhaul before returning home across the Atlantic; and

(e) during the 1920's many trawlers which had been requisitioned during the war, were refitted under the National Fishery Scheme.

A variety of warships were brought to Devonport to be completed. Amongst them were the light cruisers "Durban" and "Enterprise"; the aircraft carrier "Hermes"; the destroyer "Witch" and the submarine "L 54".

NASSA, launched 28th March 1922

WHITLEY COUNCILS

In 1916, amid serious and widespread industrial unrest, the Government set up a Committee to investigate relations between employers and employees, and to devise a way to improve those relationships after the war. This Committee, led by Mr. J.H. Whitley, M.P. for Halifax, later Speaker of the House of Commons, recommended that each industry should have joint councils of employers' associations and trade unions. These councils operating at national and district levels, would give workers a role in deciding working conditions and the principles governing the methods of fixing pay. They would also deal with grievances and consider ways of making industry more efficient through technical education and improved methods of working.

The Civil Service was not mentioned in the first Whitley Report, but the Civil Service Trade Unions and staff associations immediately saw the possibilities in the system and asked for "one of Mr. Whitley's councils". A second Whitley Report published in October, 1917, said that state and municipal authorities should form joint councils.

The Chancellor of the Exchequer, Sir Austen Chamberlain, accepted the idea in July, 1918 — but only for the Government's industrial workers. For the white-collar non-industrial staff he ruled that further thought was necessary — and set up an inter-departmental committee to consider the question.

That committee, headed by a Treasury official, reported early in April, 1919. It proposed a very modified Whitley system, a form of joint consultation without any executive powers. The committee argued that this was necessary to preserve Ministerial responsibility.

Two days later, on 8 April, 1919, the Government called a meeting at Caxton Hall to recommend the plan to civil servants. Sir Austen Chamberlain spoke for the Cabinet and urged co-operation to help remove "our old difficulties, our old misapprehensions and our old quarrels". Mr. G.H. Stuart-Bunning, speaking for the Civil Service trade unions and staff associations, turned him down. The staff, he said, were willing to co-operate, but only on equal terms; they had not even been consulted by the inter-departmental committee.

The Government agreed to joint talks. Six weeks later a constitution was agreed that gave the joint councils the right to determine conditions of service, and not merely to advise.

The Cabinet approved the revised constitution on 13 June, 1919; at a second conference on 3 July, there was an "exchange of ratification"; and on 23 July the first meeting was held of what was called "The National Council for the Administrative and Legal Departments of the Civil Service."

The Admiralty had anticipated the promulgation of the scheme of staff representation on "Whitley" lines by setting up an

Admiralty Staff Conference, which had held its first meeting on 22 January, 1919. A constitution had been agreed before the Treasury had issued its directive. When they did, the Admiralty were asked to revise theirs to conform with the model constitution.

To establish Whitley Councils in the Dockyards, a conference was held in Essex Hall, London, with Mr. Bertram Wilson of the Ministry of Labour in the chair.

The Admiralty Administrative Whitley Council held its first meeting on 21 October, 1919. Office and District Committees were then established in the Admiralty and its outposts, in conformity with a new constitution accepted in February, 1920.

Over the years, a more flexible, informal and workable system of consultation has developed. The "Whitley" machine has responded to new situations and new problems, and has developed into the cornerstone of present staff-management relations.

FIRE IN NO. 1 STORE, KEYHAM

A major fire broke out in Keyham Yard on Saturday, 15 May, 1920, in No. 1 store which formed the southern wing of a large stone building of three floors about 1,000 feet long and 50 feet high; it was erected in the 1850's alongside No. 3 Basin. Despite the efforts of sixty men of the Metropolitan Police and over 200 men from the Royal Naval Barracks, the flames fed with oil, tar and other highly inflammable material, burned fiercely for over three hours.

The cause of the fire was not discovered, but it was thought that it commenced in the part of the building where candles and other combustible materials were stored. The building had been closed at 4.45 p.m. on the Friday when the Foreman locked it and signed the 'firebook' on leaving the Yard. Nothing suspicious was noticed by the policeman who patrolled the Yard at night, and it was not until shortly before 4.30 on Saturday morning that a man on duty at Flagstaff Steps saw smoke issuing from the building.

Arising from the inquiry held after the fire, was the decision to replace the old fire engines, which had done valiant service for many years, with two up-to-date motor fire engines. The Metropolitan Police Fire Brigade had had one such engine for several years but in cases of large fires such as that in No. 1 store, it was augmented by the Plymouth and Devonport motor engines. It was realized that the local brigade might not always be available, hence the decision to obtain two more for the Met.

On 20 June, 1921 three further outbreaks of fire occurred. Two were relatively unimportant, one being an easily subdued outbreak in a submarine and the other a grass fire in the Gun Wharf ignited by sparks from the Dockyard train. This did no more damage than to burn some wooden railings, although it caused two fire engines to be diverted from a far more serious fire in South Yard.

Here, at 1.30 p.m., the alarm was raised that one of the Hemp Stores was on fire. With such a combustible store in full blaze there was little hope of saving it. The whole attention of the Fire Brigades was diverted to preventing the fire spreading to the Ropery. The Hemp Store, a two-storey building 100 yards long, was soon a mass of flames. The slender roofing collapsed, then the top floor, and tons of burning hemp and timber flooring fell upon more burning hemp. The building was practically gutted and a rough estimate of the cost was given as £20,000.

THE GEDDES "AXE"

The run-down of the Fleet after the war was not as rapid as might have been expected, because of the involvement in the War of Intervention in Russia. In April, 1921 though, questions were asked in the House of Commons whether the Government, instead of further reductions, intended to build more capital ships and whether they would be built in Royal Dockyards. The Parliamentary Secretary to the Admiralty replied that the slipways in the Dockyards were not big enough for the planned vessels and any proposal to lengthen them would not be justified during the current economic climate. It would take not less than two years, working day and night, to complete the necessary alterations, a fact which the Admiralty could not contemplate.

Sir Eric Geddes was First Lord of the Admiralty from July, 1917 until January, 1919 and became Minister of Transport in August, 1919. He relinquished that office on his appointment in August, 1921, to become Chairman of a Committee investigating national expenditure. Their report devoted about a quarter of its pages to a critical examination of Navy Estimates. It concluded

Launch of H.M.S. ADVENTURE at Devonport Dockyard, 18th June, 1924.
(Inset) Viscountess Chelmsford performing the launching ceremony.

(a) that overmanning would justify a reduction of about 35,000 officers and men from the Royal Navy;

(b) that with a smaller Navy, the Admiralty were maintaining far too large a number of shore establishments; and

(c) that the Navy Estimates for 1922-23 should be reduced from 81 to 60 million pounds.

As far as the Dockyards were concerned, the Committee reported that "the Royal Dockyards are so expensive that unless their costs can be brought more nearly to a commercial level, the work sent there should be reduced."

However, the Admiralty felt that comparisons of building costs indicated no such contrast as the Committee suggested and in the repair work, which constituted the bulk of the Dockyard work, comparison was distinctly favourable to the Dockyards.

THE WASHINGTON TREATY

Under the terms of the Washington Treaty, which was signed on 6 February, 1922, the U.S.A. offered a ten year "holiday" in capital ship construction and offered to cancel 15 such ships if

Britain and Japan took action commensurate with the American offer. The displacement of ships was also to be limited to 35,000 tons and the main armament to 16" guns. Aircraft carriers were to be limited to 27,000 tons and cruisers to 10,000 tons with 8" guns.

Britain took advantage of a clause in the Treaty though to build the two battleships "Nelson" and "Rodney."

With no possibility of building either of these ships, Devonport was fortunate in being allocated the construction of the minelayer "Adventure", the first minelayer built specifically for the purpose, all others having been adapted from other roles. "Adventure" was built originally with a square stern in which was fitted two large ports through which the mines were dropped. She served in the Atlantic Fleet from 1927 until 3 November, 1931 when she paid off into Dockyard control at Devonport to undergo a major refit, during which the square stern was altered to a round one.

An added bonus during a period of inevitable reductions in the Yard, was the work in reconstructing the aircraft carrier "Furious" — one of the largest jobs of this nature placed in any

Yard. "Furious" had been launched on 15 August, 1916 from the Armstrong Whitworth Naval Yard at Newcastle-on-Tyne. Built under the Emergency War Programme as a first class cruiser, she was designed to carry two 18" guns. Whilst building though, she was partially converted to an aircraft carrier when, in place of the forward 18" turret, a hangar was built over the forecastle with its roof forming a flight deck, 228 feet long. This enabled aircraft to take off but abaft this "flight deck" she retained the features of a cruiser. In November, 1917 she was fitted with a landing deck over her after end. It was still not a complete flight deck, because her landing and taking-off decks were separated by her bridge and funnels.

Her service with the Atlantic Fleet ended in 1919, and after a period in the Reserve Fleet at Rosyth she left in 1922 for Devonport where she was to spend the next three years undergoing major reconstruction to make her into a complete aircraft carrier.

On 1 July, 1930 she reduced to a special complement for another major re-building operation, again at Devonport. The work costing £285,354 was completed in March, 1932.

Two other ships which were originally built as cruisers, "Glorious" and "Courageous", were also converted at Devonport into aircraft carriers. "Glorious" paid off into Dockyard control at Rosyth on 14 February, 1924, but when that Yard was closed she was transferred to Devonport in 1926 — the job being completed in January, 1930. "Courageous" paid off into Dockyard control at Devonport on 27 June, 1924, and was completed and commissioned, with a Portsmouth ship's company, on 21 February, 1928.

THE FIRST DOCKYARD-BUILT CAISSON

The first caisson ever built in Devonport Dockyard was launched on 29 May, 1922 from No. 5 slip which was then still covered. It was built on its side and was intended for use at the entrance to the Prince of Wales's Basin. A similar caisson had been built at a private yard in the North of England some time earlier, but it had foundered whilst being towed to Devonport. It was then decided by the Admiralty to build one where it was needed.

FURTHER IMPROVEMENTS IN DOCK AND BASIN ACCOMMODATION

In the Navy Estimates for 1924-25, there appeared details of the cost of a new scheme for improving the docking and basin accommodation in the Yard. The main features of the scheme were the provision of a berth for a floating dock and the widening of the entrance to the Prince of Wales's Basin.

The berth for the floating dock was to be provided at the northern-most end of the Yard in Weston Mill Lake, and much dredging — at a cost of £60,000 — was required to prepare it. The dock was an ex-German one, which had previously been at Portland. It arrived in Devonport on 12 September, 1925, in tow of five tugs — "Retort", "Resolve", "St. Kitts", "St. Mellions", and "St. Clear" — and escorted by the destroyer "Tactician". After a few days alongside the Coaling Wharf, she was placed in her new berth on the 19th. Her size — 680 feet long overall and 107 feet wide between the walls — enabled any of the capital ships to be docked in her, except the battlecruiser "Hood". The first ship in the dock was the "Ramillies", who in 1920 had to be sent to Rosyth for docking because Devonport, her home port, had no suitable facilities.

The need to widen the entrance to the Prince of Wales's Basin had been made necessary because changes in the design of battleships had increased their beam, in some cases due to the "bulges" that were being added to them to improve protection against torpedo attack. These alterations had made it impossible for capital ships to enter the basin either through the direct entrance from the Hamoaze or through the Lock. This prevented them from being served by the 160 tons cantilever crane provided on the eastern side of the basin, but instead had to remain alongside the sea wall.

In the early stages little money was appropriated to this job, so it was 1929 before the work involved in widening the entrance from 95 to 125 feet — carried out by local Departmental labour — was completed.

Other schemes carried out during the period 1925-29 included extensions to the Electrical Fitters', the Joiners' and No. 81 Machine Shops in North Yard; a new entrance gate at the north end of the Yard opposite Royal Navy Avenue; a new

H.M.S. MALAYA in the floating dock 1929

motor garage to replace makeshift accommodation; a Test House for torpedo air vessels to be tested under conditions of safety; renewal of the roofs to the Quadrangle at Keyham; and a new crane track for the electrical travelling cranes on each side of No. 3 Basin.

When the Central Offices were built in 1913, no provision was made for the Superintendent Civil Engineer and his staff, so in 1930 it was decided to clear a site between the Central Offices and the Police Quarters near the gate to Keyham Yard, and to erect a brick building to replace his old offices in South Yard. The work, carried out by Messrs. Carkeek of Redruth who had also built the Central Offices, was completed in March, 1932.

THE SINKING OF H.M. SUBMARINE H 29

On Monday, 9 August, 1926, while undergoing refit in the Yard, the submarine H 29 sank with the loss of six lives. She had been exercising in No. 2 basin and was returning to the wall. Her hatches were open and her Commanding Officer, Lieutenant F.H.E. Skyrme, and some of her crew were on deck — when she suddenly heeled over and sank. The majority of men on deck were swept off and were able to swim to safety, but a Chief E.R.A. and five Dockyardmen inside the submarine were lost. As soon as word went round the Yard that H 29 had sunk, men rushed to the scene to render what assistance they could. Powerful pumps, together with the Dockyard Fire Salvage Corps, joined in the work of lowering the level of the water in the basin in which the submarine lay. It was impossible to pump the basin dry because of the other ships there, but the water was drained as low as possible. Attention was then turned to pumping water out of the submarine to put her on an even keel. Salvage was made difficult because the submarine had sunk close to the wall, making the siting of lifting lighters on each side of her almost impossible. When she was eventually salvaged and placed into dry dock, it was found that the cost to restore her to an effective unit of the Fleet would not be justified. She was therefore sold for scrap.

In September, Courts Martial were held on the Commanding Officer and the First Lieutenant,

Lieutenant M.E. Wevell. The first named was reprimanded for not taking charge of the ship and not having a clear understanding with his First Lieutenant. The latter was found guilty of negligently, or by default, hazarding the vessel, and was dismissed his ship, H.M.S. Maidstone — the submarine's depot ship — and severely reprimanded.

REDUCTIONS IN NUMBER OF EMPLOYEES

From 1926 the economic policy of the Admiralty and its direct effect on the Dockyard towns created deep apprehension at Devonport. Men over sixty years of age were discharged from the C.M., E.M., and E.E.M. Departments. One hundred other men were also discharged — or placed on compulsory leave — because of the non-delivery of material caused by a coal strike.

Employment had also to be found in southern yards for established men from the Yards at Pembroke and Rosyth which had been reduced to Care and Maintenance Parties at the end of March, 1926. Devonport received 420 men, 50% of them in the Constructive Department.

Between January, 1926 and April, 1927, over 800 men were discharged from Devonport, many ex-apprentices being amongst them. This was contrary to pre-war policy as, prior to 1914, ex-apprentices not only had preference in establishment but were assured of continuity of employment.

MORE SHIPBUILDING ALLOCATED.

After the cruiser "Devonshire" was launched in October, 1927, the slipway lay idle and a report that the Government contemplated cancelling a decision made earlier in the year to lay down three cruisers during the current financial year — including one for Devonport — caused much consternation. Various deputations waited upon the Admiralty urging the claims of their respective establishments. The outcome was that just one cruiser would be included in the following year's programme, and fortunately it would be built in Devonport.

On 1 August, 1928, the keel plate was laid and on 18 July, 1929 the ship was launched after being named "Exeter" by Lady Madden, the wife of Admiral of the Fleet Sir Charles E. Madden, Bt.

In the 1928 programme, the 10,000 tons cruiser "Northumberland" was allocated to Devonport, and ordered that she should be laid down as soon as the "Exeter" left the slip. Only preparatory work had been carried out though, when, in July 1929 Mr. Ramsay McDonald gave particulars in the House of Commons of the 'big cuts' in the naval programme. Work on the "Northumberland", and that on the "Surrey", her proposed sister ship to be built at Portsmouth, was immediately suspended and on 1 January, 1930 the orders to build them were cancelled.

SLOOP CONSTRUCTION

A surprise change in Admiralty policy brought local benefit when the building of two sloops, which had first been allocated to private yards, were re-allocated to Devonport. These sloops, "Hastings" and "Penzance", were some compensation for the loss of work on "Northumberland", and helped to dispel the gloom that had been hanging over the Yard concerning its future. They were actually laid down without ceremony at the end of July, 1929 in the Shallow Dock and after being named were floated out on 10 April, 1930.

These were the first pair of many other sloops launched at Devonport. Most were built in pairs, alongside each other on No. 4 slip — "Fowey" and "Bideford"; "Falmouth" and "Weston-super-Mare" (later re-named "Weston"); "Grimsby" and "Leith", etc. Only one other ship, "Milford" was laid down in the Shallow Dock and she was floated out on 11 June, 1932.

REFIT WORK

While orders for the laying down of new ships were always welcome, a succession of refits proved to be of equal importance. The refits of three oilers — "War Nizam", "War Hindoo" and "Orangeleaf" — proved a great boon.

One particularly major job was the extensive refit of the Chilean battleship "Almirante Latorre". She had been built at Elswick, but when completed in 1915 and war having broken out, she was taken over by the British Government and re-named "Canada". After the war she was refitted at Devonport and transferred to Chile.

In January, 1929 Dockyard officers left Devonport for Valparaiso to survey the ship preparatory to refit. Royal Dockyards did not normally undertake work for foreign

Launching Caskets for H.M. Ships Penzance (left) and Hastings

governments if it could be done by a private firm. The reconstruction of the "Almirante Latorre" was to entail the ship being in dock for a long period and at the time this could only be arranged in a Royal Dockyard. A catapult which was to be fitted in her was made in Italy, but instead of being brought to Devonport for fitting, was sent direct to Chile. The ship sailed from Devonport at the end of February, 1931.

PAID LEAVE

Leave with pay had been the aim of Dockyard workmen ever since 1920. They were being paid for just four holidays a year, and the Admiralty continued to refuse their claim that it be increased to a week. In 1929 though, the workmen were finally granted "leave with pay to the amount of one pay-week a year". In addition, the number of general paid holidays was to be increased from four to five. That extra day was taken on Boxing Day, so in 1929, for the first time, the Yard was closed on Christmas and Boxing Days and the men were paid for both. The men wanted to be able to take their week's leave when they liked, but

the Admiralty decided that the Dockyard leave must be taken during the week of August Bank holiday with Easter Monday off in lieu of August Bank Holiday.

CLOCKING-IN

The following year clocking-in and clocking-out was introduced at Devonport. The system had already been tried at Portsmouth, replacing the mustering by ticket which had been in operation for many years. The new method involved the installation of scores of clocks. At Devonport it was first introduced in the Torpedo Depot at North Yard on Monday, 8 December, 1930, where two clocks were installed. Soon afterwards it began in the Captain of Dockyard's Department and spread to all the Yard early in the New Year.

POLICE CHANGES

The Geddes Committee, in their report of 1922, criticised the policy of using Metropolitan Police to guard naval establishments and for fire brigade duties. They intimated that the cost was excessive, each policeman costing £400 per year. During the 1914-18 war, the number of Metropolitan Policemen employed in the Plymouth Division reached a total of 500. The Geddes report proposed a reduction in that number to simply enough required for the detection of crime only and that all duties of watching, gate guarding, fire brigade work and sentry duty should be carried out by active service marines or naval ratings retained for the mobilisation of the war fleet, or that a special Marine Pensioner Police Force should be set up.

In February, 1923, the Metropolitan Police ended its connection with establishments afloat when they handed over the old powder ship "Eclipse" to caretakers prior to the vessel being taken over by the Royal Marine Police. The Met. had been in charge of "Eclipse" for over 30 years and had also had charge of the "Newcastle". The two ships with their red hulls had been a familiar sight at their moorings above Saltash Bridge.

Later in the same month the Met. were replaced at the two R.N. Armament Depots, Bull Point and Gun Wharf, and in other establishments where their services were not required for the prevention of crime — but still not in the Dockyard.

Four years later the R.M. Police were installed at the Victualling Yard at Stonehouse. In consequence, Metropolitan Police officers with as much as thirteen years service locally, had to return to London, to far different duty in the streets of the Metropolis.

In January, 1934, it was decided that the Met. Police in the Dockyard would gradually be replaced. The change had already taken place at Chatham in February 1932, and at Portsmouth in August, 1932. The transfer at Devonport commenced on 13 February, 1934, when a small contingent of R.M. Police started duties at North Yard. A week later, between 20 - 30 men joined for duty at Keyham. The Met. Police were not completely withdrawn from North Yard though until 24 April.

Without ceremony, the transfer of duties from the Met. to the R.M. Police at South Yard took place at midnight on Sunday/Monday, 13/14 August, 1934, thus completely severing the connection between the Met. and Admiralty Civil Establishments in the port.

RECONSTRUCTION OF THE DOCKYARD CHAPEL

During 1930 some major reconstruction work was carried out on the Dockyard Chapel. The Admiralty helped pay for the work, although the congregation were committed to raising over £300. The Chapel, which had delightful stained glass windows and other treasures, was said to be one of only thirteen such churches of the late English Renaissance period. The peal of bells consisted of six from the foundry of John Pennington, dated 1770, and two from Messrs. Aggett's foundry dated 1868. The organ was a very fine example of the work of Master Builder Lincoln from about 1810. It had been added to in 1893 by Messrs. Hele and Sons of Plymouth, but in recent years it had suffered attack from "wood worm". At Evening Service on Sunday, 1 March, 1931 the Chaplain of the Fleet, the Ven. Archdeacon W.K. Knight-Adkin, dedicated the Chapel after the restoration had been completed.

FUTURE OF THE YARD IN DOUBT

In 1929, the question exercising the minds of Dockyard men, was "would one of the Yards be closed as surplus to requirements?" If agreement was reached between the Great Powers on the subject of disarmament, the construction of warships would be considerably curtailed. Furthermore, drastic reductions would make it impossible for the three Dockyards — Portsmouth, Chatham and Devonport — to find enough work for the large body of men employed therein. It raised additional questions, such as — in which of the three ports could the out-of-work Dockyardmen most easily be absorbed into other work? Which of the Dockyards could best undertake alternative work?

The Admiralty Joint Industrial Council invited the Dockyards to forward schemes of alternative work to avoid reductions. Proposals from Devonport included (a) the construction of a tunnel under the River Tamar — by means of a huge tube 55 feet in diameter, extending from Millbridge to Trevol, a distance of 2½ miles — which it was thought could be built for the cost of a cruiser, about £2,000,000; and (b) the construction of tanks and other mechanical equipment for the Army.

However, neither scheme was approved.

Typical Keel Laying Ceremony

Mould Loft decorated for post-launch celebrations

The local Councils of the western port continued to voice their concern for the future of the Yard. In 1933, they arranged an interview with the Admiralty and the Treasury, to make representations that a dock at Devonport should be enlarged to enable it to be used for the docking and refitting of all classes of ships. When the Keyham Extension was completed, the largest warships built up to that time could be accommodated. Subsequently, larger ships had been built, culminating with the "Hood", 41,200 tons, completed in 1920; and "Nelson" and "Rodney", 33,500 tons completed in 1927. The local facilities were improved with the arrival of the floating dock, yet the above three ships could still not be docked.

The First Lord informed the local Council that "in view of proposals made at Geneva for the reduction in size of capital ships, I think you will agree that we cannot very well embark on such a scheme."

"By the time the dock was enlarged there would be no ships of the size for which the dock was intended" said Mr. Hore Belisha, M.P. for Devonport and Financial Secretary to the Treasury.

WIDENING NO. 10 DOCK

However, three years later the Navy Estimates for the 1936-37 programme announced that No. 10 dock would after all be widened, which would permit the docking of "Nelson" and "Rodney". The estimate for the work was £345,000 but only £1,000 was to be spent in the first year. The work began in earnest in June, 1937 by which time the cost had soared to £400,000.

The widening of the dock involved the construction of a new dock wall behind the existing one, along the whole length of the eastern side. The procedure adopted was to leave the existing wall in position until the corresponding portion of the new had been built behind it.

The number of altars in the new wall was reduced from 15 to 6, and the upper section of the wall carried two cantilever cat-walks, which were to serve as positions for handling ropes, or for affording access to stagings and to the smaller vessels that may be placed in the dock.

The intermediate sill of No. 10 dock was removed, and the whole dock lengthened by

dispensing with the southern entrance. In extending the dock at its northern end, favour was given to the use of a ship caisson which did not involve the formation of a new caisson camber.

When completed early in 1939, the width of the dock had been increased by 35 feet and its length by 20 feet. It could then dock any ship in the R.N. except the "Hood", a situation which by that time was less important because she had changed her home port from Devonport to Portsmouth, where it was possible to dock her.

SABOTAGE

When the Fleet was at Invergordon, subversive elements had attempted to secure the downfall of discipline in the Royal Navy, but having been foiled, the forces of disruption turned their attention to the Dockyards.

In March, 1933, whilst the oiler "War Afridi" was in dock at Devonport, sand and brass filings were found in her machinery. In October, 1935, again at Devonport, the Royal Fleet Auxiliary "Oleander" was discovered to have nuts in her machinery, causing damage to the main circulating pump.

Early in December, 1935, it became known that further cases of sabotage had been discovered in Devonport. Serious damage had been done to the main fire-control installation of the battleship "Royal Oak", which was then nearing completion after an extensive refit. There was no possibility of the damage having been done accidentally. A sail-pin had been driven into one of the main multicored electric cables so as to produce a short circuit in the inner cables. The projecting end of the sail-pin had then been filed down and the covering of the cable carefully replaced, making detection of the cause of the fault extremely difficult.

On the same day another case of sabotage was reported in the submarine "Oberon". An iron bolt and a sheet of copper had been introduced into one of the main propelling electric motors in such a way that had they not been quickly discovered, very serious damage would have been caused to the motor. A Court of Inquiry found that the objects had been deliberately introduced into the motor.

Many other cases occurred, both in Royal Dockyards and in contractors' works. In the

Royal Yards they gradually became less serious as Special Branch officers weeded out the forces of disruption.

Sir Samuel Hoare, First Lord of the Admiralty, in the House of Commons on 27 January, 1937 stated that the acts of sabotage were instigated by a superior organisation outside the Dockyards. He vindicated the dismissal of certain men from the Royal Yards upon evidence supplied by the Special Branch of Scotland Yard.

MINESWEEPERS

Within a period of two years — October, 1936 to August, 1938 — six minesweepers were launched from South Yard: "Hebe",28 October, 1936; "Sharpshooter", 10 December, 1936; "Leda", 8 June, 1937; "Seagull", 28 October, 1937; "Bramble", 12 July, 1938; and "Britomart", 23 August, 1938.

The launch of "Seagull" was noteworthy in that she was the first all-welded ship built for the Royal Navy.

Only two of these sloops survived the Second World War — "Sharpshooter" and "Seagull". The former became a survey ship and in 1953 was renamed "Shackleton" after the famous explorer.

CRANES FOR NO. 3 SLIP

In 1937-38 the old steel "prop and job hoists" on the sides of No. 3 slip were replaced with up-to-date 30 ton electric cantilever cranes. The old steel mast hoists had been festooned with guy ropes, pulley blocks, and tackles forming a network on both sides of the slip. The nine new fixed cranes gave much clearer working space on each side and by a careful arrangement of positions and heights of these cantilevers they were able to cover the whole site. During construction of the foundations of these new cranes on the south side of the slip, the walls of the old canal were again discovered.

A completely new electrical circuit was also fitted around the area to provide improved welding facilities.

CHAPTER 16

THE SECOND WORLD WAR

In the late 1930's, Britain and France, clung to the belief that Adolf Hitler, the German Chancellor, could be placated and that the peace of Europe could be preserved. Mr. Neville Chamberlain, the British Prime Minister, flew to Germany in 1938 to negotiate with the Fuerher and returned waving aloft a copy of what proved to be Hitler's worthless pledges. As things turned out it did provide a twelve months period to improve this country's war preparations.

With the political situation deteriorating, it behove the Dockyard authorities to consider what was likely to arise if the position worsened. The Dockyard, being a vital link in the national defence, was an obvious target for air attack. Air Raid Precautions were put in hand; black-outs were organised and lessons on how to deal with incendiary bombs were given to all the staff.

When, early on 1 September, 1939, the Germans crossed the frontier of Poland — to whom Britain and France had promised certain guarantees, an ultimatum was issued to Hitler to withdraw his troops. The British ultimatum to Germany expired at 11 a.m. on Sunday, 3 September, 1939, by which time Germany had failed to comply. To the democratic Governments of Britain and France had fallen the awesome responsibility of defending the freedom of the world against Nazi domination.

Immediately on the outbreak of war, Winston Churchill was appointed First Lord of the Admiralty — a post he had held 25 years earlier. On 29 September, 1939 he made the first of his war-time visits to Devonport Dockyard.

Work in the Yard was being carried out with the utmost urgency — with day and night shifts. All types of ships were coming forward to be prepared for war — Atlantic liners, cargo boats, etc., — and the Reserve Fleet was also put into fighting trim.

The price this country was to pay was soon brought home to the people of the Westcountry with the tragic news, within two weeks of the commencement of hostilities, of the loss of the aircraft carrier "Courageous". She had left Devonport on Saturday, 16 September, with a screen of four destroyers. The next evening a

German submarine was reported, so two destroyers were detached to search for it. Unfortunately, the submarine penetrated the protective screen, and as "Courageous" altered course into the wind to land on her aircraft, she was hit amidships by torpedo. Five minutes later her Captain gave orders to abandon ship, but over 500 men lost their lives.

Then, within another month, the "Royal Oak" — the last battleship to have been built at Devonport — was torpedoed by the German submarine U47 (Lieutenant Prien). On 14 October, Prien penetrated the defences of Scapa Flow and fired a salvo of torpedoes at the anchored battleship. The "Royal Oak" capsized and sank within ten minutes with great loss of life.

War casualties soon made their appearance in the Yard — collisions, minings, and forays into difficult waters bringing more than the Yard's usual quota of work. Destroyers from convoy duties were the most regular "clients" and with the country short of destroyers and escort vessels, these had to be given priority.

About the end of 1939, H.M. King George VI paid a visit to the Yard, and he was shown the work being done in H.M.S. Adventure. In November, when three miles south east of the Tongue Light in the Thames Estuary, she had struck a mine. After temporary repair at Sheerness, she was brought to Devonport with an enormous hole in her bottom.

FRANCE CAPITULATES

Meanwhile, on the continent of Europe the Germans were overwhelming the French nation, who capitulated and signed an Armistice with Germany on 22 June, 1940.

After France had laid down her arms, Britain asked her Government to allow the French fleet to sail to British ports, thereby preventing it falling into German hands. The Armistice though, had provided that France's Navy should be transferred to German control. So, to prevent this, those French ships which were already in British held ports, were boarded and taken over.

Amongst the French warships in Devonport and Portsmouth were two old battleships "Paris" and "Courbet"; two super destroyers "Triumphant" and "Leopard"; two other destroyers, six torpedo boats, seven submarines, and several smaller units.

About 1,500 sailors and Royal Marines, and a battalion of Infantry, took part in the seizure of the French ships at Portsmouth, where things went quite smoothly. At Devonport, where there were more ships, including the "Paris" and the enormous submarine "Surcouf", even more troops took part — but events did not go so well. The ship's company of the destroyer "Mistral" opened sea cocks and tried to scuttle their ship. On 3 July, when a British party tried to board the "Surcouf" its leader Lieutenant Commander Denis Sprague, Commanding Officer of H.M. Submarine Thames, was shot dead. Lt. Cdr. Griffiths, the son of Mr. W.A. Griffiths, Secretary to the Admiral Superintendent, had been appointed a Liaison Officer to the "Surcouf" when that submarine arrived at Plymouth on 20 June. He, too, was killed, as was a Royal Marine sergeant and a French rating.

DEVONPORT-BUILT "EXETER" RETURNS HOME TO HERO'S WELCOME

It will be recalled that in the First World War, the "Invincible" and "Inflexible" left Devonport in a hurry. In August, 1939, "Exeter" found herself in a similar situation. Her ship's company were recalled from leave, to sail within 48 hours. In December, she shared with "Achilles" and "Ajax" the famous victory at the River Plate when the German pocket battleship "Admiral Graf Spee" was destroyed. The battered cruisers returned triumphantly to their home ports — the "Achilles" to New Zealand and the "Ajax" to Devonport where she arrived on 30 January, 1940. The Devonport-built "Exeter", which had suffered heavy casualties, first proceeded to the Falkland Islands to carry out temporary repairs to make her fit for the long voyage home. She arrived in Plymouth Sound on 15 February, 1940, and as the ship went up harbour, Mr. Winston Churchill took the salute as she passed the Headquarters of the Commander-in-Chief at Mount Wise. Then Churchill accompanied by Admiral Sir Dudley Pound, First Sea Lord, and Lord and Lady Astor, the Lord Mayor and Lady Mayoress of Plymouth, visited the ship in the Yard.

After an extensive refit, "Exeter" left Devonport on 24 March, 1941 — again in a hurry. She actually left before her refit was complete to avoid the heavy air raids which were then taking place on Plymouth and Devonport.

The bomb-damaged Terrace

BOMB DAMAGE IN THE YARD

The first bombs on Plymouth fell at Swilly on the first Saturday morning in July, 1940.

Plymouth continued to suffer many 'hit and run' raids, but the major devastation began on 20 March, 1941. That day, Their Majesties King George VI and Queen Elizabeth had again visited Plymouth, including the Dockyard. After an afternoon in the golden sunshine, the Royal visitors had hardly left the area before some of the heaviest raids of the war occurred on Plymouth. The following month — mainly on the 21st, 22nd, and 23rd and the 28th and 29th, the Germans' attention turned to Devonport.

The Dockyard — commanded throughout the war by Vice Admiral Arthur Ninian Dowding, who was created K.B.E. on 1 January, 1945 — became Britain's No. 1 naval repair Yard, and as such was a prime target for the enemy. It was during the heavy raids of March and April, 1941 that the heaviest damage was done in North and South Yards.

The more modern shops in North Yard were better able to withstand the attacks but amongst the buildings in South Yard to be destroyed or badly damaged were:-

The Ropery — the west ropehouse was completely destroyed, only the foundations and cellars remained; and the east ropehouse was badly damaged when about $\frac{1}{3}$rd of the building at the north end was destroyed;

The Terrace — where only two of the original thirteen houses survived;

The Mould Loft; and the Church.

The Scrieve Board was hit by many incendiaries but was saved by the gallant work of the fire-watchers — men who spent their periods of night duty in the Yard on the roofs of buildings, spotting for incendiary devices.

Old records and mementoes of the Dockyard, including a model of the ill-fated "Hood", were destroyed when No. 1 Store in South Yard was destroyed.

Damage throughout the Yard was heavy but it did not interfere seriously with the work undertaken. Only a limited amount of new construction was carried out but with the men working round the clock, a vast amount of ship repair and maintenance was done.

WARTIME ACHIEVEMENTS

The increase in the number of personnel in the Yard — about 15% — was not so great as in the First World War. Manpower was a headache, because many skilled men were sent overseas or to bases further north in the U.K., and hundreds of labourers were enlisted in to the fighting services. To ease the problem, many women were taken on to carry out a variety of jobs.

The many remarkable achievements by the men and women of Devonport Dockyard during the 1939-45 war, were disclosed in November, 1946 with the issue of the official report on the contribution of the Royal Dockyards to the country's war effort. Devonport was responsible for:-

(a) the construction of one aircraft carrier — the only aircraft carrier to have ever been built and completed in a Royal Dockyard. Launched on 30 September, 1944, as the "Terrible", she was formally handed over to the Royal Australian Navy on 16 December, 1948 and renamed "Sydney".
On 11 August, 1943 another aircraft carrier "Polyphemus" had been ordered to be built at Devonport, but this ship was never laid down and was cancelled in October, 1945.

(b) construction of the cruiser "Trinidad". Launched on 14 October, 1939 and completed on the same date two years later, her active life was destined to be short. While providing close cover to a convoy to Russia in March, 1942, she suffered serious damage from enemy shells and from one of her own torpedoes which had been fired at the enemy but then veered off course when its steering went awry. After temporary repairs at Murmansk she was again attacked on the return voyage and suffered so much further damage, that she had to be sunk by a torpedo from one of our own ships, H.M.S. Matchless on 15 May, 1942.

(c) construction of six submarines—four 'T' class patrol boats "Tudor", "Thule", "Totem" and "Truncheon" — and two 'A' class. Completion of the latter pair "Ace" and "Achates", was cancelled after their launching which took place on 14 March, 1945 and 20 September, 1945 respectively.

(d) the repair of "Exeter" and "Ajax" after their return from the famous victory at the River Plate.

(e) the almost complete reconstruction of the cruiser "Belfast". When in the Firth of Forth on 21 November, 1939, a mine exploded under her starboard side, breaking the ship's back between the bridge structure and her forward funnel. A survey of the damage was carried out at Rosyth, but that Yard was unable to undertake the major rebuilding required. In June, 1940 she sailed secretly for Devonport where she was under repair until the end of October, 1942. During this period bulges were added to her underwater shape not only to improve stability but also to add to her longitudinal strength.

(f) preparing the destroyer "Campbeltown" (ex-U.S.S. Buchanan) for an attack on the dock gates at St. Nazaire. She was fitted out in Devonport Yard between 10 - 19 March, 1942 when bullet-proof plating was fitted around her bridge; eight Oerlikon guns replaced her main armament; and torpedo tubes, depth charges and all ammunition were removed. Her two after funnels were removed and the tops of the foremost two were cut at an angle to give the ship the appearance of a German Mowe class torpedo boat. Explosives were fitted in the bows of the ship.

St. Nazaire, on the north bank of the river Loire, had the only dock — the Normandie dock — on the coast of France capable of taking the battleship "Tirpitz". After a daring entry into the harbour, escorted by Motor Launches, the "Campbeltown" rammed the dock gates and on the morning of 28 March, 1942, she exploded. The forward half of her disintegrated, and the after part ended up in the middle of the Normandie dock, carried there by the surge of water.

Although the dock was rendered unserviceable for any large German vessels, the cost of the assault in human life was high. The naval casualties were 34 officers and 157 ratings missing or killed, and the military lost 59 killed or missing and 109 taken prisoner. Only four of the eighteen M.L.'s which accompanied "Campbeltown" returned safely.

(g) disguising the "Centurion". This former battleship — launched at Devonport in 1911 — was removed from the effective list of the Navy in 1926 under the terms of the Washington Treaty. On 14 April that year, she paid off into Dockyard Control at Chatham, where she was converted to a wireless controlled Fleet Target ship.

In April, 1941 she was taken in hand at Devonport to be converted to an imitation of the King George V class battleship "Anson". The Dockyard estimated the work would take a month but it had to be done in two weeks. The work went on day and night, sometimes during heavy air raids. Her after funnel was removed, a dummy one fitted amidships and her fore one raised. Other major items fitted were three gun turrets made of wood and canvas, with wooden cylinders as gun barrels; a dummy crane and hangar; and a wooden tripod mast.

(h) the repair of the cruiser "Kent" having sustained severe torpedo damage in the Mediterranean in September, 1940. She was hit when on her way to bombard Bardia, and was towed to Alexandria by the "Nubian". She limped home via the Cape to spend nine months in Devonport Dockyard. Whilst in dock during April, 1941, she was hit by a bomb from a German aircraft, but it conveniently exploded in the vicinity of the existing damage. She recommissioned in time to join the Home Fleet at Scapa Flow in October, 1941.

(i) the war damage repair and/or refitting of over 200 destroyers in the first eighteen months of the war. A major technical job was the docking and repair of the destroyer "Javelin". On the night of 24/25 November, 1940, "Javelin" in company with "Jackal" was in action with the German destroyers "Karl Galster", "Hans Lody" and "Erich Steinbrinck", 20 miles off the Lizard. "Javelin" was torpedoed by "Hans Lody", and her bow, as far aft as her bridge, and her stern were blown off. Only 155 feet of the original 353 feet of her hull remained. She was towed to Plymouth by tug, escorted by "Kashmir", "Jupiter" and "Jersey", and she was under repair in the Yard until 28 December, 1941.

(j) the refitting and modernising of ten battleships and many cruisers. Most of Britain's best known battleships, like "King George V", "Anson" and "Howe" were at one time or other in the Yard.

Other interesting items of new construction apart from ships, were two floating docks — A.F.D. 17 and 20 — each with a lifting capacity of 2,875 tons. A.F.D. 17 saw service in Iceland before being towed to Australia at the end of the war. The dock was moored alongside Fitzroy Wharf at Cockatoo Island, Sydney, until 1964 when it was scrapped.

A.F.D. 20 was also used in Iceland, but in July 1944, it was attached to the 7th Submarine Flotilla at Rothesay. On 31 December, 1944, it sailed for Manus in the Admiralty Islands calling at Darwin, Australia on the way. When the war ended the dock returned to Singapore.

A 40 tons floating crane was made from an existing 50 tons electric travelling dockside crane which had been ordered for a foreign yard and was modified to suit its installation on to a pontoon designed and constructed by the Constructive Manager's Department.

CHAPTER 17

BEGINNING OF A NEW ERA

Two of the major private ship repair jobs carried out in the Yard after the end of World War 2 were to the 8,258 tons U.S. Lines vessel "American Farmer" and the Norwegian owned "Athel Duchess". The former vessel had been damaged in collision with her sister ship "William J. Riddle" on 31 July, 1946 when 700 miles west of the Lizard. She was brought in to Falmouth where a 40ft. patch was secured over the hole in her side. After discharging her cargo at Southampton she returned to Devonport on 11 October. The repairs were completed 22 days inside the contract period of 70 days, completing, by coincidence, on American Thanksgiving Day, 28 November.

The "Athel Duchess", a 13,000 tons tanker, 500 feet long and 63 feet beam, had been damaged by a mine in the Bay of Biscay. She broke in two but the stern portion was taken to South Wales and beached. There she lay partly submerged until being towed to Devonport Dockyard in December, 1946. The Yard had undertaken, at a fixed price contract of £250,000, the engineering feat of constructing and fixing a new fore end and repairing the after end.

The new fore end was laid down on 26 March, 1947 and launched 9 December, 1947 by Mrs. Hvistendahl, the wife of the Norwegian owner. Work was in hand until June, 1948 during which time the costs rose to over £420,000. For nearly twelve months the Admiralty tried without success to secure a contribution from the ship's owners to off-set the loss. The Admiralty had been most anxious at the time to secure "repayment work" in order to use the Dockyard resources to the full and maintain employment. When charges such as interest on capital, dock rental and wharfage were taken into account, and the fact that overhead expenses of at least £100,000 would have continued even if the order had not been accepted, the nett loss was no more than about £40,000.

MORE POLICE CHANGES

During the 1939-45 war, the R.M. Police had been supplemented by the R.M. Police Special Reserve. Even with these two forces there was still not enough manpower for duty at all the establishments in the United Kingdom, so a third force, the Admiralty Civil Police was introduced. This situation of having three forces remained until October, 1949, when they were all disbanded and the Admiralty Constabulary was formed.

They reverted to the Metropolitan style of policing and new recruits were sent to a Training School where they were taught law, regulations, etc. They acquired modern techniques, had radio vehicles, pocket radios, etc., and their own Criminal Investigation Department.

The Air Ministry and War Department had their own Police Forces, but when the three Service Ministries came together under the title of Ministry of Defence, it was decided to amalgamate the three Police Forces into one single force to be named the Ministry of Defence Police. The changeover took place on 1 October, 1971.

FURTHER DOCKYARD EXTENSION

After the war, concern was expressed at the apparent lack of any decision at the Admiralty concerning the expansion and development of Devonport Dockyard. In November, 1946, they asked Plymouth City Council to acquire 182 acres of Devonport. Within three years though, the Admiralty revised its intentions, when they announced that in the next twelve years they would only need 154 acres. The next year, their demands were almost halved — just 78½ acres — but it still meant that about 3,500 people would have to be re-housed.

In March, 1955, the Admiralty released 17 acres, the reduction being thought due to modern warfare's need to avoid excessive industrial concentration. Two years later they gave up another 10 acres, by which time a new wall — ultimately to be about 400 feet long — was under construction around the perimeter of the extended Dockyard.

South Yard was extended eastwards to Chapel Street, including most of Fore Street and southward to Duke and Duncan Streets; and Keyham Yard was extended almost to Devonport Park between Albert and Ferry Roads.

A "NEW" DOCKYARD CHURCH

During the wartime blitz on the area in April, 1941, the Dockyard Chapel was destroyed. From then until 1957 services were held in the Church Hall in South Yard. In 1956 the Admiralty decided to restore the Kelly College Mission of St. Chad, which stood in Moon Street, Morice Town, but after the post-war expansion came within the Dockyard wall.

The foundation stone of this Kelly College Mission, for the ground floor only, had been laid on 18 June, 1900 by the C. in C., Plymouth, Admiral the Rt. Hon. Lord Charles T.D.M. Scott, K.C.B.

The ground floor was completed and, on 2 October, 1901 was dedicated by the Bishop of Crediton. The rest of the Church was erected over it as funds became available.

On 17 August, 1909 the foundation stone of a permanent Chapel of St. Chad was laid on the ground floor by Lady St. Levan, and on 1 March, 1910, under the patronage and title of St. Chad, was dedicated again by the Bishop of Crediton. The last service held in St. Chad's took place at Christmas, 1954. The building became Admiralty property soon afterwards and the ground floor was used as a Church Hall for the Dockyard from the Spring of 1955.

On 7 June, 1957, the Church, after a full restoration, was re-dedicated "to the Glory of God and in Honour of St. Lo" as the Royal Dockyard Church of Devonport by the Lord Bishop of Plymouth, Rt. Rev. Norman Clarke, LlD, assisted by the Ven. Archdeacon Frederick Darrell Bunt, O.B.E., M.A., Chaplain of the Fleet.

In the wall of the present Church have been mounted the inscribed plaque of 1700; and the foundation stones which were laid in 1900 and 1909. The first named item was found, in 1957, in 98 pieces but was restored by the C.E.M. Department.

On 30 October, 1972 an Industrial Mission Centre was opened in the basement of the Church, brought about by a unique agreement between the Royal Navy and the Diocese of Exeter to cover the "parish" of the Dockyard and St. Aubyn's outside. It was formally opened by the Port Admiral Devonport, Vice Admiral John McKaig, and was afterwards blessed by the Archdeacon of Plymouth, Ven. Frederick Matthews.

GOSCHEN YARD

In the 1950's the Dockyard extended into an area at Keyham where once stood, before the wartime blitz destroyed them — Goschen and Hamilton Streets, and Spencer Avenue. In 1957 the first half of a new Main Electrical Factory was completed there. At the opening of the second half in 1963 by the then Admiral Superintendent, Vice Admiral G.D.A. Gregory, he asked the electricians for a name for this new extension. They chose Goschen Yard after the name of one of the former streets, which itself had been named after Mr. Joachim Goschen, afterwards Lord Goschen, who in 1871 had been First Lord of the Admiralty.

INTERNAL COMBUSTION ENGINE (I.C.E.) SHOP

In 1940-41 an I.C.E. Repair Depot was established at Harrowbeer — remote from the Dockyard target area — to deal with the engines of M.T.B.'s, etc. To relieve post-war congestion in the Quadrangle, the Dockyard absorbed the former R.N.E.C. workshop. Some shops moved to Goschen Yard, but the small I.C.E. Section was moved to the north of No. 5 Basin.

On Friday, 4 October, 1963, a new I.C.E. shop — a purpose built workshop covering 11,000 square feet and costing £65,000 — was opened in Goschen Yard by Vice Admiral G.D.A. Gregory. First projected in 1953, it was the first new major workshop to be opened for the Engineering Department since 1955.

POST-WAR SHIPBUILDING

The first warship to be built at Devonport after the Second World War was the "Salisbury" — the first of a new type air direction frigate — and the first all-welded ship to be built at Devonport on the pre-fabricated principle. She was launched on 25 June, 1953, almost eight years after the war ended. Over the next fifteen years, five more frigates were launched — "Plymouth" on 20 July 1959; "Tartar" on 19 September, 1960; "Cleopatra" on 1 March, 1964; "Danae" on 21 October, 1965; and "Scylla" on 8 August, 1968. Six frigates in fifteen years shows the reduction in the amount of shipbuilding when compared with the period 1900-14 when ten battleships, two battlecruisers and three cruisers were launched.

This reduction meant frequent slack periods on the building slips. To help tide the Dockyard over one 'sticky' period, it was announced in December, 1963 that the Yard would build three 200 tons Dumb Lighters. At the time some men — including shipwrights, blacksmiths, welders and burners — were being paid without any work to do. As the lighters had no engines, their construction would not make demands on Departments already fully employed.

With the launching of "Scylla" some people considered that the building of ships in Devonport Dockyard had come to an end. However, on 22 June, 1970, the keel-laying ceremony of a Research and Development Vessel, RDV O1, took place when the first weldment was placed in

Setting-up of SCYLLA prior to launch

Launch of SCYLLA

position by eighteen women "manning" the capstan bars. These wives of Dockyard officials and Trade Union representatives clocked on for the job and received one penny and a souvenir ash tray as their wages. A pay-slip in their wage packet read:- Rate for the job 6/-; less 2/- tax, 8d. insurance and 3/3d. for the cost of the ash tray. The launching ceremony on No. 3 slip took place on 20 March, 1971, when Mrs. Wildish, wife of Vice-Admiral D.B.H. Wildish, named the vessel "Crystal". High winds prevented the actual launch that day, but the vessel eventually took to the water on 22 March. Costing about £2¼ million, this floating laboratory was the first of her type to be built for naval underwater research. Flat-bottomed and without engines, rudder or armament, she was 414 feet long and displaced 3,246 tons. Her hull was penetrated by shafts so that various devices could be submerged from her.

The "Crystal" left Plymouth under tow on 13 December, 1971 for Portland where she provided the Admiralty Underwater Weapons Establishment with a stable platform on which to carry out acoustic tests.

As the "Crystal" entered the water at her launch, the first weldment of a Naval Armament Lighter was swung by crane into position on the slip. Five weeks later three of these 200 tons Lighters were completed. Each comprised five weldments which had been fabricated in No. 4 Machine Shop and assembled on the slipway.

The next construction jobs were two 290 tons Fresh Water Lighters. Towards the end of 1972 work on a 1,100 tons Caisson commenced on No. 3 slip. About 760 tons of structure were involved, prefabricated in the shops and assembled on the slip. It was built as a spare for No. 5 Basin or No. 10 Dock at a cost of £500,000, and was launched at 1830 on Monday, 30 July, 1973.

Concurrently with the Caisson, further up the slip, a Dumb Tank Cleaning Vessel was also being assembled. The combined work on this T.C.V. and the Caisson was almost equivalent to the hull structure of a frigate and kept 100 men employed for six months.

In May, 1974 the Dumb Tank Cleaning Vessel, TCL 02, moved off No. 3 slip. It was the first of its kind and one of a programme of six — three of which were built at Devonport. They provided full tank-cleaning facilities for H.M. Ships with accommodation for three officers, seven crew and ten cleaners.

A purpose-built electrical test barge, MAC 1013, was launched in February, 1975 at a cost of £500,000. It had a remote control system with a larger capacity to test main generators than existing load barges. It was used to good purpose on "Fearless" where six generators were tested with minimum disturbance to other ship activities. It is also capable of being used to test generators on nuclear submarines.

The possibility of warship construction being reintroduced to Portsmouth and Devonport Dockyards was reviewed by a Headquarters Working Party in 1978. It had been set up by the Chief Executive Dockyards, Mr. Harold Chatten, who asked the two Dockyard General Managers, Mr. William Seward (Portsmouth) and Mr. Keith Thomas (Devonport) to let him have their comments and proposals.

Mr. Thomas commented: "Despite the major development at Devonport for refitting ships in the future, everyone would welcome the opportunity to again undertake the building of new ships. Devonport has a proud record of new construction and over the years has built up a great deal of expertise with modern frigates. It is to be hoped that, if any decision is taken to build new ships at Devonport, it will be before that expertise is lost. Some improvements will need to be made, of course, to our building slip and other facilities if we are to build any new ships economically."

The following year though, it seemed that the building of ships of any size at Devonport really had come to an end. Why? The cantilever cranes which before World War 2 had been erected on each side of the main slip, No. 3, were being removed. One of them, No. 352, had been dismantled in 1971 and re-erected in the Royal Maritime Auxiliary Service complex in Morice Yard. Then on 23 April, 1979 men of the Yard Services Manager's Department commenced cutting down seven more of the cranes. The last surviving crane, No. 308, was sold for scrap to Marple and Gillott of Sheffield, in June, 1981.

By now the shipbuilding area of the Yard was almost non-existent, with No. 3 slipway looking rather a forlorn sight when compared with its former glory. Only two support frameworks to the cantilever cranes still survive — one on each side of the slip. No. 4 slip, once used for building two sloops at a time, is still in use but simply for hauling up small craft. The Mould Loft is built over what was once No. 5 slip, and between the last named two slips stands the Scrieve Board. Built over the original No. 2 (later No. 4) slip, its floor is no longer in any fit state for laying off ship's lines.

Once again then, the question is being asked — "Has warship building at Devonport come to an end"? As long ago as 1929 many people answered the same question with an emphatic "Yes". They were proved wrong and who knows that the present day pessimists may not again be proved wrong. Conventional shipbuilding would prove difficult with so many facilities having been dispensed with, but with modern methods — who knows? Might weldments be assembled — in workshops or on docksides — and these be assembled into ship form in a dock? Only time will tell.

MODERNISATIONS AND REFITS OF AIRCRAFT CARRIERS

Between the Wars, the Dockyard employees were grateful for the work involved in the conversions of "Furious", "Glorious" and "Courageous" into aircraft carriers. For twenty years or more from 1956 onwards, the Dockyard economics were again very much dependant on work in the modern generation of aircraft carriers.

The modernisation of "Centaur" during the period 1956-58 was the Dockyard's first large scale experiment in "planning". It proved so successful that the Yard was able to meet the completion date originally estimated.

The "Eagle" and "Ark Royal" were regular visitors to the Yard for varying length refit periods. A four year modernisation period for "Eagle" began in the spring of 1960, during which time she was fitted with a fully angled flight deck; two steam catapults replaced the hydraulic ones; and new flight deck armour to enable her to operate Scimitar and Sea Vixen aircraft. More than 3,000 men were employed, and the cost of the modernisation was £30 million.

"Ark Royal" had been refitted in Devonport in 1959 — when her side-lift was removed — and in 1961 — when deck landing projector sights and more powerful steam catapults were installed. In October, 1966, a three year £30 million modernisation commenced — "a task of staggering magnitude" — to enable her to operate Phantom aircraft. Preparatory work had begun in the Yard about two years earlier.

Another multi-million pound project occurred with the conversion of "Hermes" into a Commando Carrier. The fixed wing capabilities such as catapults and arrester gear were removed. An innovation as far as Devonport was concerned was the building of a Bailey Bridge from the dock side to the flight deck to allow vehicles to drive on and off. It was built as a training exercise by a unit of the Royal Engineers.

DOCKYARD SCHOOL

During the 1941 blitz, the School buildings in South Yard were destroyed. The apprentices though, continued their studies at Montpelier School and in St. James' Church Hall and School.

In 1952 the Dockyard School occupied part of the R.N.E. College at Keyham, and a few years later took over the whole building when its title was changed to the Dockyard Technical College.

From 1905 the School had been divided by examination results into Upper and Lower streams. If students in the Lower School failed to reach a satisfactory standard, they then stopped going to School. Very few boys were able to complete the full four years' course.

In the late 1950's the Upper/Lower School system was replaced by three parallel paths through Higher/Ordinary National Certificates; City and Guilds of London Technician Courses; and Craft Courses. All apprentices had release time from their trade training to attend courses — two days for the higher levels and one day for the less academic.

The 1944 Education Act had ruled that it was the responsibility of Local Education Authorities to provide "further education". In December, 1970, it was revealed that formal negotiations had been going on between the Ministry of Defence and Plymouth Corporation to agree terms and conditions for transfer of responsibility for Devonport Dockyard Technical College to the Local Education Authority. The transfer took place in the following year. The R.N.E. College continued to be used although Craft and Technician Courses were conducted in the local College of Further Education, and H.N.C. Courses in Naval Architecture in Plymouth Polytechnic.

RIVER-SIDE FLYOVER

A flyover built along the riverside between North, Morice and South Yards, meant that the three Yards virtually became one, and obviated the need to go out of the Dockyard to get from one Yard to another. It also helped enormously with transport within the Yards and contributed to the ending of the Dockyard's internal train service. The passenger service had boasted at least six classes ranging from The Admiral, Principal Officers to Labourers. This "class distinction" was forgotten on Monday, 16 May, 1966 when the last passengers were carried.

A Dockyard passenger bus service was then introduced using 36 seater coaches. Bristol K5 G double decker buses were introduced on 1 December, 1969 — four on Dockyard service and two for the movement of naval ratings. These buses were gradually replaced with Leyland Atlantean double deckers.

A much reduced rail service, handling goods only, continued until 10 November, 1982. On that date, more than 100 years of tradition ended when the last train passed through the tunnel from South to North. There it was met by the Port Admiral, Devonport, Vice Admiral David Brown, who took from the driver, Mr. Dave Rogers, the key that the locomotive had carried on every journey, and which ensured that only one train was going through the tunnel at any one time.

Farewell to the Dockyard Railway

Dockyard Crest

DOCKYARD CREST

On 15 June, 1964, the Admiral Superintendent, A.J. Cawthra, wrote to the Second Permanent Under Secretary of State (Royal Navy) suggesting the creation of a badge for the Dockyard, based on the disused Arms of the former Borough of Devonport.

From information received from the Ships' Badges Committee and advice from the College of Arms, the new design was approved and introduced in February, 1966. In heraldic terms it is described thus:- "Per fess, white and blue, a foul anchor proper between two dolphins heads downwards and facing inwards blue and in the base, the frame of a ship also proper."

NEW CENTRAL OFFICES

In November, 1964, work began on new Central Offices — a three storey glass and reinforced concrete building — on land then used as a car park. It also took in part of old William Street which had been closed since 1959.

The Offices were designed by the Ministry of Public Buildings and Works, and built by Messrs. Humphreys Ltd., of Plymouth. The ground level covered an area of 34,364 sq. ft., but because of its cantilever construction, the top floor had an even bigger area.

The building was to provide accommodation for about 700 Dockyard staff, bringing together under one roof, departments which had been scattered around the Yard. The combined Drawing Offices, the S.N.S.O.'s Department and the Finance Manager's machine section began their move into the new offices on Thursday, 29 September, 1966 and was completed by the Sunday.

On Trafalgar Day, 21 October, 1966, Mr. D.W. Smithers, Director of Dockyards, in the presence of the Lord Mayor and Lady Mayoress of Plymouth, unveiled a plaque to open formally the £460,000 first stage.

Phase Two, a 110 feet high block, ten storeys high, was officially taken over from the contractors on 21 July, 1970.

ALBERT ROAD GATE CLOSED

The Albert Road entrance to Keyham Steam Yard was closed for the last time at midnight on 4 September, 1966. With a new Dockyard wall being built around the extended Dockyard, the opportunity was taken to re-site the gate. The towers remained, but the Dockyard clock, fitted with a new electrical movement, was moved from its original tower to the other nearer the road.

APPRENTICES TRAINING CENTRE

In June, 1967, work commenced in Goschen Yard on the construction of an Apprentices Training Centre. The plan had germinated several years earlier when it became apparent there would be a need for centralising apprenticeship training. Designed by the Ministry of Public Buildings and Works and built by Staverton Ltd. of Totnes, it was opened in January, 1970.

GIRL APPRENTICES

In 1970 an attempt to attract girls to take up apprenticeships in the Yard flopped badly. For the first time the Yard was to open its doors to girl apprentices, for electrical work in particular. Sixty enquiries were received but only nine girls completed the application forms. Seven of them sat the examination and six passed. Four who were successful in the Craft examination decided after all not to enter the Yard. Two girls passed the Technicians examination, but one failed the interview. The remaining girl passed the interview and was offered entry, subject to certain G.C.E.

'O' level passes — which, unfortunately, she failed to achieve.

In September of the following year though, girl apprentices did enter the Yard for the first time. Twenty three applied for the examination; twenty one sat it; fourteen passed, of which eight took the opportunity of being trained alongside 230 boys.

THE DOCKYARD FIRE BRIGADE

An Admiralty Working Party had been set up in 1959 to review the organisation of the Admiralty Fire Services in Britain. This Party recommended the gradual withdrawal of Brigades, leaving the Dockyards to rely on local authorities.

The Dockyard Fire Brigade had been manned by the Metropolitan Police followed until 1939 by the Royal Marine Police. At the outbreak of war, full-time manning was adopted, using naval reservists. In early 1941, the Royal Naval Fire Force was introduced under the control of Fire Officers appointed to the staff of the local C. in C., and comprising serving professional firemen (mainly reservists) and new entry stoker ratings. During 1944, nine appliances were manned on a full time basis with ten more manned during silent hours and on a 'Red' alert at other times. All stations of the Fire Force were controlled from watchrooms staffed by the Women's Royal Naval Service.

At the end of the War, the R.N. Fire Force was disbanded and the R.M. Police again manned the appliances. Watchkeeping by volunteers was introduced in 1948 and continued after the integration of the R.M. Police and the Admiralty Constabulary. Manpower was later reduced, first to one crew for both Yards and then to a smaller appliance with less men.

The Dockyard Fire Brigade was finally disbanded in 1968 and the Yard is now protected by the local authority's Fire Brigade. The redundant fire station at Albert Road gate provided a site for another Dockyard Museum. Its predecessor — in the Adelaide Gallery between Nos. 2 and 3 docks in South Yard — was destroyed in the fire of 1840. This latest Museum was officially opened on 28 April, 1969, by Mr. Basil Greenhill, C.M.G., Director of the National Maritime Museum at Greenwich. It did not remain there for long though, but was moved to the former Guard House inside the Fore Street gate to South Yard when the Albert Road gate area was re-designed.

DOCKYARD NEWSPAPER

A scheme for a monthly Dockyard newspaper was introduced "for the benefit of all employees and their families, and to tell the local community something of the Dockyard's many achievements." Dr. David Owen, Parliamentary Under Secretary of State for the Navy, and M.P. for the Sutton Constituency of Plymouth, said he hoped "it would improve communications throughout all levels of management and workpeople.

Chatham Dockyard launched the scheme with "Periscope" in 1966, and was so successful that the other Yards followed suit; "Trident" at Portsmouth; "Spotlight" at Rosyth; and "Devonport News" at Devonport, the first edition of which was published on 29 January, 1969. It consisted of twelve pages and cost 4d.

CHAPTER 18

A TEN YEAR DEVELOPMENT PLAN

In October, 1966, the appointment was announced of a General Manager for Devonport Dockyard. He was Captain H.G. Southwood, who at the time was Manager of the Engineering Department at Portsmouth Yard. His first task, after taking up his new duties on 30 January, 1967, was to plan the formation of an entirely new Dockyard management structure on a functional basis. Devonport was the last of the four Royal Yards to adopt this 'new look'.

Traditional titles like M.C.D. (Manager of the Constructive Department), M.E.D. (Manager of the Engineering Department) and E.E.M. (Electrical Engineering Manager) passed into history. The General Manager was to have a team of five Managers, each in charge of his own Department to carry out the Dockyard's main task of refitting the modern Royal Navy.

A Production Department — responsible for repair and new construction — would have its own constructive, engineering and electrical divisions;

A Control Division — to ensure proper progress of work;

A Planning Department — which already existed in embryo in the Yard Planning Office;

A Yard Services Department — which looked after cranes, dock pumps and electrical power, but had to be knit into a single organisation; and

A Finance Department which was already in being, having been formed from the old Cashier's and Expense Accounts Officer's Department.

Additionally, a Personnel Department was to supervise the entry, training, promotion, welfare, etc., of the industral and non-industrial work force.

Mr. L. Kirkpatrick, O.B.E., R.C.N.C., was the first Production Manager and was succeeded by Mr. F.W. Matthews, M.R.I.N.A., R.C.N.C., so that after more than a century the responsibility for 'engineering' within the Dockyard reverted to a Constructor Officer.

The Defence Budget of 1968-69 made a commitment to modernise, type and redevelop the principal bases of the Royal Navy at Devonport, Portsmouth, Chatham, Rosyth, Portland, and the Clyde. Unlike the spasmodic and piecemeal growth which had taken place over the last century, the new development was to be pursued in a logical sequence and in accordance with long term development plans.

At this time, however, three new factors were also stressing the need for co-ordinated development. Firstly, the Dockyard Review under Rear Admiral J.D. Trythall had proposed the 'typing' of classes of different ships to different Yards, with the Leander frigates and their successors, Types 21 and 22, falling to Devonport. Secondly, Devonport had been selected as an operational base for nuclear submarines and as a support base for their docking, refitting and refuelling. Thirdly, with the withdrawal from overseas bases, the need had been established for an improvement to the naval support which U.K. could provide for ships under self and assisted, maintenance when away from home ports.

In 1969, a small team was formed under the leadership of Mr. B.J. Hoskin, Assistant Yard Services Manager, to evaluate costs and to prepare basic designs for three major projects — a Typed Frigate Complex, improved nuclear facilities and a Fleet Maintenance Base. The following year three separate teams — one for each project — were formed.

Admiral D.B.H. Wildish, then A.S., Devonport, obtained the C. in C., Plymouth's approval to call in the other Devonport authorities — Commodore, R.N. Barracks; Captain, Fleet Maintenance; and P.S.T.O.(N) — to produce an overall plan for the development of Devonport as a Fleet Base. In 1970 the Plan, in principle, was approved by the Admiralty Board, and henceforth Devonport Dockyard became known as the Devonport Naval Base.

CHIEF EXECUTIVE, ROYAL DOCKYARDS

A key factor in plans to modernise and streamline the Royal Yards and make them more efficient was the formation of a new post — Chief Executive, Royal Dockyards. The details were announced by Mr. D. Healey, Secretary of State for Defence, and Mr. Leslie W. Norfolk took up the appointment at Bath on 2 September, 1969.

The Minister's approval of proposals put forward by Mr. Norfolk in December, 1969 and March, 1970 led the headquarters at Bath to prepare a Dockyard Management Plan, by means of which Headquarters and Dockyards would be able to guide their management development activities. A Consultative Committee on Dockyard Management was formed and they first met in 1972.

THE MALLABAR COMMITTEE

A Committee under the Chairmanship of Sir John Mallabar, was appointed on 19th December, 1968

"to examine whether the existing organisation, systems of control and accountability of large scale establishments in the Ministries of Defence and Technology engaged in production, offer impediments to the achievement of full efficiency, and to recommend how such impediments should be removed."

After a two and a half year inquiry, their report covering the Royal Dockyards was presented to Parliament in July, 1971.

Much on which they reported had been

overtaken by events; important changes in the top structure of the organisation in the Ministry of Defence concerned with the operation of the Dockyards and the support of the Fleet had already taken place or were in prospect. Predictably, the Committee endorsed the appointment of Mr. Leslie Norfolk as Chief Executive of the Royal Dockyards, and decided the title "Admiral Superintendent" should be eliminated, "Flag Officer" becoming the sole title.

The Committee came down firmly against 'hiving off' the Dockyards to private enterprise but left no doubt that it was time they were put on a commercial basis and freed, as far as possible, from the tight grip of the Navy.

"As a spur to efficiency" said the report "there should, where possible, be greater competition with outside yards. This might lead to reconsideration of the overall capacity required. Should a decision be taken to reduce capacity appreciably, it would be preferable to close one dockyard which might be sold off for other purposes rather than continue with four under-used Yards."

Mr. David Howell, Minister for the Civil Service, announced in the House of Commons on 15 July, 1971, that the Government accepted the broad principles of the recommendation and was considering how best to implement them.

The next month, when Mr. Peter Kirk, Defence Under Secretary for the Navy, met M.P.s from Dockyard constituencies, in the House of Commons, he gave them a firm assurance that no naval repair work would be contracted out to private yards, and that all four Royal Yards were safe into the foreseeable future.

INTRODUCTION OF THE TITLE "PORT ADMIRAL"

When Vice Admiral Sir Charles Mills completed his appointment as Commander in Chief, Plymouth on 28 May, 1969 his successor acceded to the new title Flag Officer, Plymouth.

The first to hold the appointment was Rear Admiral John Roxburgh, but only temporarily. Four months later Vice Admiral Anthony T.F.G. Griffin took over. In April, 1970 he also assumed the additional role of Superintendent of the Dockyard, thus ending the Dockyard's separate command which had existed since 1691.

On 15 September, 1971 Flag Officers of the Royal Navy who had also borne the title "Admiral Superintendent" were re-styled "Port Admirals". The change in the title was consistent with the recommendations made in the Second Report of the Mallabar Committee on Government Industrial Establishments that the title "Admiral Superintendent" should be eliminated. The change also reflected developments in the organisation and management of the various facilities at the main bases. On the one hand, the responsibilities of General Managers of Dockyards had increased; on the other, a wider "Naval Base" concept had developed under which the Port Admiral was required to control and co-ordinate a wide range of base support activities.

THE SUBMARINE REFIT COMPLEX

On 7 October, 1969 it was announced by Dr. David Owen, the Navy Minister, that a new operational base for the support of nuclear powered submarines was to be developed at Devonport.

First steps to meet the nuclear commitment was the conversion of North Lock into two separate docks, Nos. 11 and 12. The contractors, Tarmac Ltd., started work in December, 1970 by building a ferro-concrete dividing wall. No. 11 was to be made capable of taking an SSN (nuclear fleet submarine) and No. 12 could also dock one, if required, by fitting a ship caisson instead of a sliding type. The cradles for SSNs were fitted off centre to allow conventional centre-line blocks to remain installed, thus minimising the time required to change the function of the docks.

Early in 1972, the development of the North Lock area was completed; No. 11 dock was flooded for trials and a week later the conventional submarine "Otus" was the first docked therein. The first time a nuclear submarine was docked was when "Valiant" entered No. 12 dock in December, 1972.

These two docks, Nos. 11 and 12, were supplemented by the Admiralty Floating Dock 58 which had been brought round from Portsmouth and berthed to the east of the promontory in No. 5 Basin. Together they provided the necessary dock replacements for Nos. 5, 6 and 7 docks, which were out of use whilst the Frigate Complex was being built.

H.M.S. ONSLAUGHT in A.F.D. 58

In June, 1972 demolition of buildings between North Lock and No. 10 dock started to allow contractors to move on to the site to build a line of Docking Support Buildings. The whole area was enclosed within a security fence and so arranged that one or both docks could be isolated for either nuclear or conventional work. This enabled Devonport to meet any nuclear docking commitment and to do most work on an SSN, but not with the intensity required during refit. For this much greater involvement, the main Nuclear Complex was built in the north west corner of No. 5 Basin.

The building of this Complex provided a formidable task for the architects, Howell, Killick, Partridge and Amis; for the consulting engineers, Sir Alexander Gibb and Partners; for the builders, French Kier; for the Property Services Agency; and for the Ministry of Defence (Navy) team. The result of this amalgam of design, building and engineering skills, is the best submarine refit facility in the whole of Europe.

The basic plan was to build a 280 feet wide promontory centrally between the existing arm in No. 5 Basin and the west wall, which was to be flanked on its east and west sides by two docks, Nos. 14 and 15. The contractors for Stage 1 were Messrs. Costains Ltd., who started work in October, 1973, the first task being to provide a dry site by removing the water from the basin, the first time it had been done since the basin was first flooded in 1906. To accomplish this a cofferdam was built between the southern end of the existing arm and the west wall of the basin north of the sliding caisson. The basin walls had to be strengthened to ensure that when the water was removed, the walls did not collapse under pressure from the water left on the other side.

Work on Stage 2 which embraced the actual construction of the Complex, including the two dry docks, began in 1975 and was undertaken by Messrs. French Kier Ltd.

The docks, instead of being fitted with the conventional caissons, are provided with flap gates which hinge at the bottom and lie flat on the bed of the basin when open. They were made in Glasgow and delivered to the site by sea. These two docks were primarily for SSN refitting, but are long enough for the emergency docking of SSBNs (nuclear powered ballastic missile submarines). They could also be used for docking frigates if the programme allowed, or required it.

Dominating the Submarine Refit Complex is a giant 80 ton cantilever crane. It is centrally placed on four massive concrete columns, which straddle a service road and plunge to the depths of the complex. These supports also form the framework for large water storage tanks. The main structure of the crane was built by Redpath, Dorman Long and the cantilever and main machinery was designed and constructed on site by the crane division of Stoddart and Pitt of Bath. The £2½ million crane has a radius of 72 metres maximum and 15.5 metres minimum and is capable of lifting the specially designed used core packages weighing about 72 tonnes across No. 14 dock to a rail transporter.

The main buildings are situated between the two dry docks with almost as much accommodation below their apparent ground level as above. The eight storey central management office is at the landward end of the Complex. In the middle is the submarine support facility comprising nine storeys — five above and four below. At the southern end are the three storey project control offices and the ready-use workshops.

Pumping out and flooding of the docks, and the raising and lowering of the dock gates is remotely controlled from the Control Centre.

The Submarine Refit Complex was officially opened by H.R.H. Prince Charles on 23 May, 1980; and blessed by the Bishop of Plymouth, Rt. Rev. R.F. Cartwright.

The task of planning the preparation of the Submarine Refit Complex for the first refit was vested in a S.R.C. Working Party. It consisted of representatives of the Planning, Yard Services, Production, Nuclear Power, and Naval Stores Departments. Also represented were the Staff side and Trade Unions.

Even so, the refit of the first, "Swiftsure", was not without its problems. Scheduled to commence in 1979, the start was delayed through labour disputes. Eventually the Dockyard management reached an interim agreement with the Trade Unions, and preliminary work on "Swiftsure" began on 7 February, 1980. It was later found necessary to extend the refit period because of a number of technical and procedural difficulties encountered as the management sought to gain the necessary experience. It was also found that the wrong welding procedures had been used in the nuclear reactor primary cooling system. As a result, extensive pipe lagging had to be stripped off before the correct welding could be done.

"Swiftsure" completed her major refuelling refit in March, 1983. The last stages of the refit went particularly well, with power range testing being completed in record time, and sea trials conducted without a major hitch.

During the year April 1982-March, 1983, Devonport consolidated its position as the Fleet's major submarine refitting Yard with the commencement of dual streams of SSN refuelling refits and SSK refits with "Sovereign", "Conqueror", "Opportune" and "Olympus" all in hand.

THE FLEET MAINTENANCE BASE

From October, 1967, the Captain, Fleet Maintenance was accommodated in H.M.S. "Tyne", berthed on the north arm of No. 5 Basin, providing workshops and accommodation for the Fleet and Craft Maintenance Groups. The arrival of the nuclear submarines in 1972 required specialised support which "Tyne" could not provide, so "Forth", which had the necessary facilities, was brought back from Singapore, given a short refit, and commissioned in February, 1972 as H.M.S. Defiance berthed on No. 8 wharf. This ship was also found not to have the capacity to cope with the growing number of ships and submarines requiring shore-side support, so a new

Submarine Refit Complex looking westward

H.M.S. SOVEREIGN in the Refit Complex

The Fleet Maintenance Base

F.M. Base was built on shore in close proximity to the Submarine Refit Complex. It was to provide new mechanical and electrical engineering repair facilities; stores for equipment; command offices, etc. In the principal workshop, the repair and refit of ship's mechanical items, electrical components and electronic gear can be carried out; periscopes are refitted; and in a vertical tower alongside, periscopes can be raised, tested and calibrated. On the north side are two and three storey high ships' command offices; and overlooking the North Quay are the ships' stores, located in a single storey "supermarket" building.

In this Fleet Maintenance Base area, a new jetty - to provide additional berths - was built in Weston Mill Lake, connected by a bridge to the foreshore of the R.N. Barracks, H.M.S. Drake.

The F.M.B. was opened by the Prime Minister, Rt. Hon. James Callaghan, M.P. on 21 April, 1978.

TYPED FRIGATE COMPLEX

In January, 1970, Dr. David Owen, Parliamentary Under Secretary of State for Defence (Navy) announced a further modernisation plan for Devonport Naval Base which was to include the covering of three docks - a plan which scotched rumours and removed all doubts on the future of the Yard. The area chosen for development was No. 2 Basin and Nos. 5, 6 and 7 docks at Keyham.

The first stage of the work, to provide a new and unrestricted access to the site for the main contractors, was completed in March, 1972. To provide such an access required reclaiming land by filling in Moon Cove.

The new development was originally named the "Leander Frigate Complex" and coincidentally the isolation of the area occurred when H.M.S. Leander, after refit, was undocked from No. 7 dock - the last ship refitted in the area under the old system.

The organisations mainly concerned with the detail, design and construction were the Property Services Agency for the docks, basins, subways, etc.; Sir Alexander Gibbs and Partners, consultants for the dock coverings and other buildings; and Kier Ltd., the main contractors.

Work commenced in earnest in the autumn of 1972 when power and telephone cables were re-routed around the east sides of the old 5, 6 and 7 docks to leave the development site clear. Cofferdams were built across the tideway entrance to No. 2 Basin and across the caisson gap between Nos. 2 and 3 Basins, so enabling the former basin to be pumped out.

The existing entrance lock had to be removed; the south wall partially re-aligned; and a new entrance made slightly north of its original position to improve berthing facilities. The south side wall was cut back and straightened to provide a stripping-out berth on the south side clear of other ships coming in to dock. The old promontory of the south lock was removed and the inner west wall refurbished to provide a fitting-out berth. The complete closure of the gap between Nos. 2 and 3 Basins provided a third berth to the north end of No. 2 Basin as well as a comparable berth on the other side of the wall in No. 3.

During the construction period, access to the basin floor was gained by temporary ramps, which were removed prior to the final flooding of the basin on completion. The stone excavated was used to reclaim mud flats in Camel's Head Creek.

The dock entrances are closed by "Box" falling leaf type gates which open into the basin, where they are housed in pits at basin floor level to allow the ships to pass over them. A similar gate is provided at the basin entrance where there is also a traditional ship caisson.

A very flexible pumping system has been provided in the underground pump-house between Nos. 5 and 6 docks, which controls not only the flooding and emptying of the docks but also the water level in the basin. The docks can be partially flooded from the river or by transferring water between them before levelling off by connection with the basin. Emptying the docks is normally achieved by pumping the water into the basin but it can also be done in part by discharging into the river if the tidal level is suitable.

Cranage in the basin is provided by four fixed tower cranes - three $12\frac{1}{2}$ tons and one 50 tons to provide a heavy lift on the sea wall. Cranes running each side of the docks provide full coverage up to 20 tons and are supplemented by 5 tons radio-controlled hoist blocks in each ridge of the docks' covers, to deal with high level lifts from ships.

Workshops, stores, etc. are provided together with offices and general amenities for a workforce of some 200 non-industrials and 1200 industrial employees.

The main feature of the project though was the covering of the docks - emulating the feature first proposed in 1812 by Richard Pering. Rising to an overall height of 160 feet, the doorway entrance is 130 feet which gives about 25 feet clearance over the top of a frigate entering the docks. This allows for any future expansion of radar displays at mastheads.

The doors are based on a Swedish design and consist of four large sections which are pulled up at different speeds to arrive at the top of the support columns together. They are also capable of independent operation to allow the upper section to be lowered for ventilation.

On 1st August, 1974, the Complex was accidentally flooded when the cofferdam across the entrance sprang a leak. Over 100 men worked throughout the night to fight the flooding which covered the two acre site to a depth of six feet, damaging contractor's plant and materials. The cause of flooding was believed to have been a fault in the rock below the main entrance in the cofferdam.

The first official flooding of the Complex took place on 2 June, 1976. Water gushed into No. 2 basin, through the balancing culvert, to a depth of three feet. Six days later the basin and three docks were fully flooded. Trials were carried out in March, 1977 when the first ship "Galatea" entered. On 2 May, 1977, the Complex began its working life with the docking of "Cleopatra" in No. 7 dock. After undocking, she was then used to

115

Accidental flooding of the Frigate Complex site

commission No. 6 dock on 30 May before being berthed on the west wall of No. 2 basin. Finally No. 5 dock was commissioned on 26 July when the "Active" was brought in for a Tilt Test. Due to a dock not being available elsewhere in the Yard, No. 7 dock was used on 14 July - using a docking cradle - for a final refit docking of "Olympus", the first submarine in the Complex.

On 23 September, 1977, the Complex was formally opened by Dr. David Owen, M.P. when a demonstration docking of "Galatea" took place; she entered No. 6 Dock to a musical accompaniment provided by the Royal Marine Band.

Within the first year's life of the Frigate Complex, 27 docking operations took place, including 5 Leander class frigates and 2 Type 21's, "Antelope" and "Ambuscade".

Ships entering the Complex for normal refit are piped and wired into full supplies of firemain; steam; chilled water for electronic cooling and air-conditioning; L.P. air; electricity; and sewage disposal, thus enabling the ship's company to live, sleep and eat on board normally throughout the refit.

In January, 1981, trials were carried out in No. 6 dock to test a theory that would enable that dock - without major construction work - to accept one of the first batch of Type 42 destroyers. It was thought to be too expensive to excavate through the concrete floor and bed rock to provide for the profile of those ships, so the idea was put forward that the depth of water in basin and dock be increased. It had been proved possible to bring the water in the basin up to the required depth, but the problem was that a higher

116

water level in the dock would penetrate the service inlets around the sides. Blanking plates were therefore designed and fitted.

Approximately 23,000 tons of water were then pumped into No.6 dock to test its strength and watertightness. The result was successful and no leakage occurred in the galleries. The only remaining requirement would be the building of the higher centre line dock block arrangement.

As yet though - a type 42 destroyer has not been docked in the Frigate Complex.

OTHER MAJOR CHANGES IN FACILITIES

In June, 1967 Richard Costain (Construction) Ltd., began work on two storehouses, a steel framed building for paints and acids, 200 feet long x 100 feet wide x 22 feet high; and a similar building for the storage of cables, 180 x 80 x 28 feet.

Four months later in South Yard, an office block was built for the Ministry of Public Buildings and Works. A dozen apprentices helped in the construction of this two storey building, which with 2,700 square feet of floor space housed both technical and clerical staff.

March, 1971 saw the opening of a new £285,000 restaurant, which replaced the old one, whose site

Frigate Complex opening ceremony

Frigate Complex with H.M.S. GALATEA entering the basin

was required for workshop development. Contractors for the new building were Dudley Coles Ltd.; engineers, Clarke Nichols and Marcel; and architects, Devereux, Mitchell, Price Davies and Bertram Carter. Two storeys high, North Restaurant, as it was named, was designed to "feed" food and stores to satellite restaurants and kiosks in other parts of the Yard.

At the end of 1971 an announcement was made of various new building projects, costing £20 million, that were to take place between then and 1975. They included the modernisation of No. 3 Machine Shop to provide it with pre-fabrication facilities; modernisation of Nos. 79 and 81 shops for light plate work; improved ships' storing and de-storing facilities; provision of crane tracks at No. 1 basin; extension to No. 3 wharf; and improvements to 5, 6 and 7 wharves.

In April, 1972 a £160,000 Yard Services Workshop in North Yard was accepted by the Yard Services Manager, Captain J.C. Frederick, R.N. The building 250 feet long, 55 feet wide and 36 feet high, was completed three months ahead of schedule. It had an office block at its southern end and an amenity centre with lockers for 200 men. It replaced numerous sub-standard makeshift premises scattered throughout the Yard and brought widely varied activities under one roof. This workshop was first planned to be built on a site at Moon Cove where the old Welding Repair shop stood, but that area was absorbed into the Frigate Complex project. The new site was chosen between the Frigate Complex and the Submarine Refit Complex, and close to the normal ship repair areas in North Yard.

Improvements were also taking place elsewhere in the Naval Base, particularly in the workshop and storage areas. In addition to modernisation, a process of rationalisation, i.e. the combination of similar processes in the same area, was adopted. Plate work was being centralised into two main areas; one for light plate work and the other for heavy plate.

For the woodworkers, an extension was to be built on to the Joiners Shop, east of No. 5 Basin, and this with the original shop refurbished, would hold all centralised woodworking tasks, and also the textile workers (carpets, curtains, upholsterers, etc.) and the Life Raft and Safety Equipment Sections from the old Torpedo Factory and Morice Yard.

Drawings were produced in 1971 by Sir Alexander Gibbs and partners for a new Pipe Shop to be erected in North Yard on the site formerly occupied by a Gunmounting Shop. It necessitated alterations to the British Railway's entry into the Yard and the moving of railway sidings. Constructed by Balfour Beatty and various other sub-contractors, the Pipe Shop, 169 metres long, 54 metres wide, and 15 metres high, was completed in 1975. Moving in began on 17 March, and the shop was officially opened by the Chief of Fleet Support, Vice Admiral P. White, C.B.E., on 16 June. It brought together the Coppersmiths from the Engineering Department and the Plumbers and Coppersmiths from the Constructive Department.

A purpose-built Medical Centre was built next to the St. Levan Restaurant, close to St. Levan Gate, North Yard. It opened on 5 November, 1979 as the Occupational Health Centre. The antiquated Medical Centre in South Yard was to continue to provide treatment facilities for employees in that area, but a location for a new Centre was to be earmarked in the South Yard Development Area.

On the site of the old Dockyard School behind the Medical Centre in South Yard were built offices for the Small Ships Section Headquarters. The two storey building - built to accommodate a staff of 50 - cost £44,000 and was completed in May, 1979. The Small Ship Section, which deals with any ship smaller than a frigate, was previously housed in scattered wooden huts, the condemned York Street School, the old Devonport Market - to mention just a few - which created problems of co-ordination.

A Glass Re-inforced Plastic Shop was also built in South Yard, where GRP processes were tried out for the better use of such material in all Yards.

NAVAL STORES DEPARTMENT

The first major storehouse to be completed in the Dockyard's reconstruction programme was opened on 5 February, 1963 by Mr. F.C. Wilkins, Director of Stores. Built in the former Fore Street area of Devonport - which had been cleared by the wartime blitz - it was the start of the Naval Stores Department's realisation of gathering their activities into a single storekeeping unit. Other buildings were erected for the storage of a vast range of equipment comprising electrical, electronic and general stores, supported by Receiving and Issuing Centres, and an Outward Shipping Store.

Then on 12 June, 1980 the largest storehouse - 85,000 square feet of storage space on four floors - was officially opened by Mr. R.J. Thornton, Director General Naval Stores and Transport. He unveiled a plaque commemorating the opening of this Fore Street Stage 4 building, which had been built by Marples, Ridgway at a cost of £1½ million.

INDUSTRIAL ACTION

The 1970's saw much industrial action in the Yard. There had been a mass one-day stoppage amongst the workforce in August, 1969, but Devonport's first recorded industrial action at officer level occurred on 16 April, 1970, when 68 instructors walked out from the Apprentices Training Centre in Goschen Yard. They were demanding to be regraded as Civilian Instructors and to receive an extra £4 a week - a claim which they were later granted.

Two years later, much more industrial action over pay occurred in the Yard - token strikes, withdrawal of labour - culminating with official strike action which began on 25 September, and brought the Naval Base to a halt. On 3 October though, the men returned to work.

In the later years of the 1970's, Civil Servants went on strike - a walk-out from the Yard which affected several ship refits. In June, 1979 the Yard was again almost at a standstill.

LARGEST ALUMINIUM MOULD EVER BUILT IN THE U.K.

On 17 January, 1975, a major achievement by Devonport Naval Base workers went on show to the press - the first and largest aluminium mould built anywhere in this country. It had been prepared in the new fabrication bay in No. 3 Machine Shop, for the G.R.P. Mine Counter-measure vessel H.M.S. Brecon to be built at Vosper, Thornycroft's Yard at Woolston, Southampton. As the mould was 200 feet in length, it was taken, in sections, by ship to Southampton.

"CRADLE" DOCKING

Further progress towards the greater flexibility and improved use of docking facilities was made in October, 1976 with the cradle docking of H.M. Submarine Rorqual in No. 10 dock - the first time with a conventional submarine in a Royal Yard, and also the first time No. 10 dock had been so used.

Blocks were made in the Machine Shop, South Yard, delivered to No. 10 dock, and positioned six each side of centre line. The final fitting of soft wood capping was done in situ to ensure a tailored fitting to "Rorqual's" hull.

The success of the operation ensured a saving in dock space leading to the possibility of cradle docking submarines side by side and considerably increasing the potential in the Naval Base's role in submarine refitting.

EMERGENCY AT NO. 2 DOCK

On 22 September, 1980, surface cracks were noticed in the granite setts holding the caisson at the entrance to No. 2 Dock, South Yard. After a night of heavy rain and winds, water was trickling into the dock which contained the R.M.A.S. tug "Advice", halfway through a refit.

A watch was maintained and as the danger intensified, the Department of the Environment officials decided that the granite blocks would not hold out against the pressure of another tide.

To avoid possible risk of life, action was hurriedly taken to prepare for the emergency undocking of "Advice". Between 6.45 p.m. and 4 a.m. the next morning, No. 2 dock was the scene of great activity. Demarcation lines were ignored, so that by 8 a.m. "Advice" had been undocked and moved to No. 4 basin in North Yard.

At low tide the crack in the dock wall was a horrifying sight and divers reported that granite blocks had shifted as much as 8 inches.

The repairs took six months to complete, after which the first ship to enter the dock was the survey ship "Hecla".

NEW ENTRANCE TO THE NAVAL BASE

The shift of emphasis to the north end of the Naval Base, with the Submarine Refit Complex and the Fleet Maintenance Base, raised the question of a new access to the Base from the north. The volume of contractors' traffic made it obvious that the existing gate at St. Levan Road could not cope. A new access was therefore built, with a road coming off the public road system near the junction of Saltash and Wolseley Roads, across reclaimed land, round the seaward side of H.M.S. Drake, on to a new embankment and so into the Base.

IN-DEPTH STUDY OF THE ROYAL DOCKYARDS

In September, 1979, the Secretary of State for Defence, Francis Pym, called for various studies on defence, one of which was an in-depth study of the Royal Dockyards. The Dockyard Study was carried out under the direction of a Steering Group chaired by Mr. K. Speed, Parliamentary Under-Secretary of State for the Royal Navy, and a Working Group led by Mr. M.J.V. Bell, Head of the Management Services (Organisation) Division, Ministry of Defence.

Their Terms of Reference read:—

"A Study is to be undertaken of the role, organisation and structure of the Royal Dockyards in the United Kingdom. It is to consider how the Royal Dockyards might best be organised to meet the requirements of the Royal Navy in the 1980's and 1990's."

"It should take full account of the level and nature of the capacity elsewhere in British Industry for ship repair. The Study should assess the cost and manpower implications of any changes that might be recommended, with particular reference to the position that would obtain at 1 April, 1982."

The Steering Group visited all four home dockyards and three of British Shipbuilders' yards; and sought evidence from all who might contribute to the Study. They aimed to identify the main problems, to suggest a framework for solutions and to propose a programme for further work. They stated "the difficulties of the Dockyards will not be easily or quickly resolved. If confidence is to be restored, there must be a clear strategy for the future applied consistently over time."

Some of the main features of the Report, which was published in two volumes, entitled "The Royal Dockyards; a framework for the future", included:—

(a) explanations that there was a crisis in the Dockyards. This stemmed from the decline in the capacity of the Dockyards to meet the needs of the Navy, the inability of Dock-

yard managers to respond to the problems they perceive and loss of confidence among the workforce.

(b) detailing the problems they had identified and their proposals for changes;

(c) summarising the measures they believed necessary to overcome the crisis in the Dockyards. In particular, Dockyard management needed to be given more freedom to manage resources, including earnings and manpower, and in return be held accountable for its performance against firm objectives; and

(d) concluding that substantial, albeit unquantifiable, savings in money and manpower should be realisable from improvements in Dockyard efficiency and streamlining Dockyard management.

The report recommended that an early announcement should be made about the future of the four home Dockyards. The Government had accepted the recommendation in the Report, and confirmed the need to retain the four Yards, though levels of employment in each Dockyard would depend on the success of their management and workforce in improving efficiency.

Within a few months though the Government's intentions were drastically revised.

CUTS IN DEFENCE SPENDING

In January, 1981, Mr. John Nott, Secretary of State for Defence, announced huge cuts in defence spending. In his speech on the Defence White Paper, Mr. Nott said that as well as a reduction in manpower, there would be comparable cuts in materiel. Britain's contribution to the N.A.T.O. naval effort was to be reduced from 59 surface ships to 50 - with some ships being put in the standby fleet as part of this commitment.

The main cuts announced were:—

(a) at least one of the brand new "Invincible" class aircraft carriers. At the time "Invincible" was ready to come into service, "Illustrious" was building; and "Ark Royal" had just been laid down. The ship thought most likely to be axed was the "Invincible". (It was subsequently announced that "Invincible" was to be sold to Australia).

(b) the assault ships "Intrepid" and "Fearless";

(c) the entire Rothesay class of frigates.

(d) most of the County class missile destroyers;

(e) some of the Leander class frigates;

(f) "Hermes", the last of the fixed wing carriers would end her career in 1983, three years before her time;

(g) "Endurance", the Antarctic Survey Support Ship; and

(h) at least four Royal Fleet Auxiliary ships.

A decision was also taken to close Chatham Dockyard, with its nuclear submarine refit facilities, and to reduce Portsmouth Dockyard to a minor repair Yard. This would leave just Devonport and Rosyth to maintain the entire fleet. It meant that Devonport was to become the undisputed home of the Royal Navy, with enough work to keep the Yard fully employed for many years to come and with a probable addition of 1,500 extra staff - some of whom would be transferred from Chatham and Portsmouth.

Once again though plans had to be changed; this time as a result of events that took place thousands of miles away in the South Atlantic.

THE FALKLANDS CAMPAIGN

In March, 1982, an illegal landing by 60 Argentinian scrap merchants on South Georgia Island, 800 miles southeast of the Falkland Islands, angered Great Britain. They had landed from a cargo ship under the pretence of collecting scrap metal from a dis-used whaling and sealing station at Leith, but once ashore they hoisted their nation's flag. Argentina escalated the problem when their armed forces invaded the Falklands.

Many diplomatic exchanges took place but with Argentine's refusal to withdraw her forces, Britain's patience was exhausted. "Operation Corporate" was mounted in remarkably quick time, and an armada of naval ships and auxiliaries assembled at Portsmouth to sail for the South Atlantic on 5 April, 1982.

National publicity focused on Portsmouth, but the sending of this Task Force also meant a considerable amount of work for the men and women of Devonport.

Devonport Naval Base had the aura of a factory at war. Demarcation lines were forgotten amidst the frantic activity preparing naval and commercial ships. Quite magnificent feats were accomplished on board the ferries, container, and

roll-on/roll-off ships, converting them into aircraft transports and support ships.

The first to arrive at Devonport - Cunard's 18,000 ton R.O./R.O. container ship "Atlantic Conveyor", chartered by the Ministry of Defence to carry Harrier jump jets to the Falklands - was completed in 9 days. After a Harrier trial landing on board with the ship in the Sound, she sailed south on 25 April.

Another Cunarder "Atlantic Causeway" had her decks strengthened, and a month's work was done in 8 days. British Telecom's cable-laying ship "Iris" was fitted with a strengthened helicopter pad. She arrived at Devonport at ten o'clock at night, but the work started at once and was completed within 4 days.

The Sealink ferry "St. Edmund", within 7 days, had two large landing platforms welded to her with the appropriate strengthening of structure in the vicinity. The "Contender Bezant" had a series of raised hatches with gaps which needed to be filled in. Her after hatch was strengthened to provide a landing area; and ramps were constructed to the storage area. A large hangar was also built.

The turn-round time for the conversion and storing of other ships was equally as impressive, and included "Rangatira", 22 days; "Laertes", 10 days; "Astronomer", 9 days; and "Wimpey Sea Horse", 2 days.

Although there was so much work going on at home, there was no shortage of volunteers from Dockyard men to make up a small Dockyard Repair Group to go to the South Atlantic and carry out hull repairs on the spot.

The Argentine forces in the Falklands surrendered at 9 p.m. on 14 June, 1982. Tears, cheers, music and banners greeted the return home of ships, some of them battle scarred and needing repair. Regrettably some ships did not return. The Devonport ships "Ardent" and "Antelope" and the Container Ship "Atlantic Conveyor" were lost during four disastrous days towards the end of May.

CONVERSION TO NORTH SEA GAS

In June, 1982 discussions started on supplying North Sea gas to Hill 60 Boiler House, which supplies heating to many areas of the Yard. With

ATLANTIC CAUSEWAY – a hive of activity

an estimated saving of £200,000 per annum, it will have paid for the conversion within twelve months. Devonport was the first Yard to take advantage of the scheme — "Interrupted Tariff" — which means the price of gas will be linked to, but always cheaper than, furnace fuel oil. After conversion, the three boilers will be able to use gas or oil.

The contract was placed on 3 November, 1982, and conversion work on the first boiler began on 24 January, 1983. As one boiler was fired on gas, work commenced on the next, until all three were converted.

CHAPTER 19

BUILDING FOR THE FUTURE

During the summer of 1982, the development of facilities in Devonport Naval Base took off again following a lean period resulting from the financial restraints imposed by the Government prior to the Defence Review in 1981. During this period, work identified in the Naval Base Development Plan as being necessary to update existing facilities had been suspended.

A Study was undertaken late in 1981 by the Naval Base Development Organisation to identify specific projects considered to be essential by the General Manager and other Port Admiral's support Managers. This limited new programme of works, identified as the "Way Forward Programme", covered the transfer of indirect ship work from Chatham and Portsmouth and the refitting and support of new classes of ships not previously allocated to Devonport. It was considered to be the essential minimum programme required to meet the future.

These projects ranged from the installation of large numbers of machine tools (particularly in the Quadrangle); provision of additional test rig facilities in the Combined Weapon Equipment Workshop; improvements in the Goschen Yard Electrical Factory and Weapons Radio Factory; to improvement to some amenity centres and extra office accommodation for Design Division staff.

Other improvements to slips, basins and other afloat facilities in various part of the Yard were approved together with a substantial extension to the Non-Destructive Testing Centre.

Approval was also given to build a jetty, off the shore-line between Nos. 3 and 4 slips in South Yard, to support the Testing and Tuning of weapon systems by the operational fleet and the storage and embarkation of lubricating oil. The two year contract, worth £2.3 million, was awarded to Cementation Construction. Work began in December, 1982 on the 130 metre long reinforced concrete jetty supported by tubular steel piles, which will be capable of accommodating the new Type 22 frigates and other ships up to 4,000 tons displacement. The contract excluded the cost of dredging which had taken place in 1979. The Jetty is expected to be completed in 1985 and handed over to the Yard Services Manager for the provision of services.

Other tasks given the 'go ahead' were:—
(a) improvements to the staff amenities in PSTO(N)'s motor transport complex;
(b) provision of permanent accommodation in the Submarine Refit Complex to meet the expanded nuclear submarine programme;
(c) provision of modernised fleet facilities at the head of No. 10 dock; and
(d) the building of two large additional stores in South Yard in support of PSTO(N)'s enhanced tasks.

MEETING FUTURE POWER DEMANDS

The face of the Dockyard was expected to visibly change during 1983 to meet its future power demands. The old Dockyard Power Station is nearing the end of its life, so a new Central Frequency Changer Station is to be constructed on the site of the Tamar Brewery. The new Station will be the hub of the power system developments designed to meet the demands of the 21st century. It will convert the South Western Electricity Board's intake at a frequency of 50Hz to the 60Hz

Site of the new Central Frequency Changer Station

used by warships; and will distribute and control all the electricity used in the Base.

Other facilities will have to be moved; the Yard Services Mobile Crane Pound will be moved to Morice Yard; and the Yard Services Scaffold Store and Production Manager's Pipe Lay-apart Store will be moved to the old East Ropery building in South Yard, thereby making effective use of this historic building.

The construction of the new Central Frequency Changer Station on the brewery site, together with the installation of equipment and modifications to power distribution systems, will be a long and complicated task which has to be planned to minimise disruption to the Naval Base. It is hoped to have the first new frequency changers operational in 1986.

A new 33,000 volt sub-station will also be built in Goschen Yard.

"THE DOCKYARD OF THE FUTURE"

£150 million have been spent on the Devonport Naval Base over the past 20 years (1962-82) and a further £45-£50 million is to be spent on major works over the next 6 years; making it the largest dockyard in Western Europe.

Improvements planned include more offices, a new high voltage distribution system for the nuclear submarine refit programme and more improvements to increase surface ship refit capacity.

The Government's decision to keep the carrier "Invincible", the assault ships "Fearless" and "Intrepid", and the missile destroyers "Bristol", "Fife" and "Glamorgan" instead of selling or scrapping them over the next two years, will mean a much bigger work-load for Devonport.

Defence Secretary John Nott's plans to boost Britain's defences in a £1 billion package was expected to bring several hundred more jobs to Devonport.

In January, 1983, the Dockyard General Manager, Mr. Jack Bedbrook, stated that "the current salary and wages bill for the year is £109 million and is expected to rise to £120 million in 1984. The workforce would grow to 13,600 by April, 1984."

"The Dockyard's role in the support and maintenance of the Fleet has assumed major proportions. The Frigate and Submarine Complexes are constantly in use. At any one time thirty ships and submarines could be in the Dockyard for refit and repair. More may be berthed alongside needing Dockyard help during their operational time."

"Devonport Dockyard was in the spotlight last year during the Falklands crisis. As one of the two remaining Dockyards it is likely to stay in the public eye in the future. We must therefore build on our successes of the past year and show everyone that we are not taking the future for granted — that way we can ensure that Devonport is recognised as the Dockyard of the Future."

May that future follow the motto of the old Borough of Devonport.

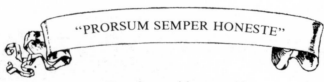

"PRORSUM SEMPER HONESTE"

Ever forward honourably

FROM COAL TO NUCLEAR POWER

Dockyard Coal Wharf looking south 1960s

Submarine Refit Complex looking north 1980s

Where it all began — No.1 Dock and Wet Basin centre foreground